Copyright © 2019 by Savannah Moore-Stein
All rights reserved. This book or any portion thereof may not be reproduced or used in any manner whatsoever without the express written permission of the publisher except for the use of brief quotations in a book review.

Printed in the United States of America

First Printing, 2019
ISBN 9780578453248

Village Books Publishing
1200 11th St,
Bellingham, WA 98225

www.Villagebooks.com

DID I RAISE YOU RIGHT?

A Single Mother's Memoir

SAVANNAH MOORE-STEIN

To my beautiful daughter, Mari, thank you for letting me expose our life together. May you realize and know your light within and let it shine!
I love you bunches & gobs!

To Rand, my incredible husband, thank you for your love and support. You bring me such joy!
I love you so!

FOREWORD

"We don't develop courage by being happy every day.
We develop it by surviving difficult times and
challenging adversity."

~ *Barbara De Angelis*

This is one woman's life story of courage in learning to face adversity and continue loving, caring and learning despite the difficulties. Her story is not centered around extraordinary events; you will find no terrorist suicide bombers, no armed gunmen spraying bullets and no genocidal warriors marching through these pages. What you will find is the all-too-common and heart-breaking events that so many of us have had to face with extraordinary courage as parents, caregivers and those who experience deep loss – of innocence, of people we love and even, in the dark night of the soul, ourselves for a time. Fundamentally, this memoir asks the questions out loud that many of us are asking of ourselves inwardly. Did I do enough – for my child, my parent, my partner and myself? Was my grief too much or too little? Did I live according to my highest understanding of integrity, or did I fail to do that, and either way, could I have lived in a way that alleviated suffering more fully for those I love? These are remarkable and uncomfortable questions, questions that deserve to be considered in our own lives. Perhaps this is the greatest gift of a memoir – to invite us in to the author's own deliberation on these central questions so that we ask them of ourselves.
The Rev. Dr. Andrea Asebedo, D.D.

INTRODUCTION

I believe that when a subject touches your soul, you should share it. I've always felt drawn to write a book but ignored my interest in doing so until now. I told my now-husband that I wanted to write a book; but I had no idea about what. While listening to an amazing lesson from our minister one Sunday, the words "Did I raise you right?" came to me. That was my "aha" moment, providing me with the answer: write a book about a concern I've carried all my daughter's life. I knew this was what I must do, because as I talked about this book, I cried. This is a memoir of my life while raising my daughter as a single mother. I have written this book in hope of touching someone's life. I know raising my child alone is not unique. But my daughter experienced some horrific ordeals as a child and young adult. Over the years, I've avoided thinking about those things because to know how much pain she's experienced has caused me pain as well. I've essentially tried to avoid that pain all these years. Now I've cracked open that pain to investigate my guilt in all this. I was her mother, the only person she could trust; and I felt I didn't protect her. I'm hoping that writing this book will be cathartic for me and for my daughter. And I hope others may relate to what I've felt as a parent about whether I've really raised my daughter right.

TABLE OF CONTENTS

1. ....My Early Life
2. ....Our Child is Born
3. ....Many Changes
4. ....Friends
5. ....What to Do?
6. ....Back on Track
7. ....A Big Birthday
8. ....New Life
9. ....A Good Marriage
10. ....Ahh....the Beach
11. ....Meanwhile She Keeps Dancing
12. ....Our Time by the Lake
13. ....Her Grandpa
14. ....Functioning
15. ....Lonnie
16. ....Alone
17. ....Our Wedding(s)
18. ....Retirement
19. ....Happiness for Mari?
20. ....Her Dad's Family
21. ....It's Not Over
22. ....What's the answer?

CHAPTER 1

My Early Life

I was born to two loving, wonderful parents in upstate New York. I remember bits and pieces of my childhood in Syracuse until we moved when I was six years old. I had a good childhood. My sister Beth and I were raised in a strict but loving way. I always felt loved and secure, knowing that my parents loved each other and loved Beth and me just as much. I was very lucky to have such wonderful parents.

I have fond memories of my childhood. I remember watching Howdy Doody and Mickey Mouse on TV in a small apartment my parents rented before my sister was born, nearly 3 years later. I can remember a few trips, one even by train, to Schenectady to visit with my mother's sister and my favorite aunt, Jane. My parents owned a Plymouth. It had a huge back seat that Beth and I could easily fall asleep in the back on our trips to visit relatives; and we did sleep often on these trips. My parents took us a few times to see our new house being built; and I very clearly remember the smell of fresh wood. I love that smell to this day.

Beth and I played fairly well together, even though we fought often. We played with the kids in the neighborhood when we moved into our new house, which was on a cul de sac.

MY EARLY LIFE

We had lots of room to play on our safe street. One of the many very cold winters, the neighborhood kids came over to ice skate in our backyard. Dad filled the backyard with water which froze overnight into a perfect skating rink! We had so much fun. My dad padded Beth and me with pillows, strapped on our backs with rope, so that we would have a 'soft landing' when we fell on our bottoms.

I remember my awesome kindergarten classroom, which consisted mostly of toys and a play area with a play kitchen. I remember how much fun I had playing there. The school was one big building, with a mud room for us to hang our coats up when we came in. The kids in our cul-de-sac all rode the school bus; and one day a third-grade boy sat next to me on the bus and tried to kiss me. I was so embarrassed! I was sure that everyone on the bus was laughing at me. I felt awkward and uncomfortable, and rather helpless in the situation. This third grader's move was certainly unwelcomed. Odd the things we encounter as children that stick with us.

My parents dealt with some difficulties in raising my sister and me. My sister was the child who was always getting hurt. I mean really hurt, like nearly cutting her heel off (just missing her Achilles tendon) while riding on the back of the bike; also getting hit in the head with a baseball one day at school; falling off a high wall and cracking her skull open on the concrete below requiring many, many stitches and resulting in a concussion.

She could have been killed or brain damaged from that fall on her head and ended up very lucky. I teased Beth about being 'brain damaged' after that. I loved to tease her.

One day a neighbor's dog bit Beth. She was still very little. It wasn't really a bad bite; probably just a nip. But the dog owners were so upset that this happened. My parents worked it out with the owners, saying it was ok – not as bad as everyone might have thought – and took Beth to the doctor to make sure she was ok. Beth was not afraid of dogs after that. But I was, even though I wasn't the one that the dog bit. Another situation of a childhood memory that upset me and created a fear.

I was the one who was always sick. I was born with asthma and I had to use an inhaler a lot. The inhaler was made of glass in those days. I had to be very careful to never drop it. I can remember being in the hospital with pneumonia for a long time when I was only two years old, with an oxygen tent around me. It was traumatic for me. My parents were not there with me at night. The hospital just didn't allow parents to stay in the hospital with their children at that time. I'm sure I remember this time, even though I was only two, because it was so traumatic for me to be without my parents. I was afraid of the dark, felt abandoned; and I have this memory in my mind to this day, even though my parents didn't actually abandon me while I was in the hospital.

MY EARLY LIFE

My parents were most concerned and attentive to my health. I've thought about that situation over the years, about how I felt alone for so many nights – like my parents had just left me. Many things can leave a mark, even as deep as a scar perhaps, on a child's life many times without a parent being aware of it.

My mother was a stay-at-home mom most of our childhood. She was strict, more than my dad; but she was loving, especially when it came to taking care of me. I can remember being home from school many times because of severe breathing problems due to my asthma. My mother would fix me warm meals, sit on the couch and watch TV with me - anything to make sure I was ok. My father was the parent who 'fussed' over us. He was very loving, kind and generous, almost to a fault. He would have given the shirt off his back to a total stranger. But he was also very protective of 'his girls', sometimes worrying too much about things.

I inherited many fears from my dad that I am still working to shed. I also inherited some wonderful qualities from both my parents. Beth and I were taught to be polite and to speak and eat with proper manners. Our parents were not stuffy; I'm sure that's just the way parents raised children then. I spoke my mind, even at a young age. I was strong-willed and opinionated; and I was often, within polite boundaries, allowed to participate in some adult conversations. Beth, on the other hand, was shy and quiet. Throughout my childhood my parents mentioned often how smart I was.

Beth was told by our parents, and other adults, how cute she was. As adults, Beth and I have discussed how this shaped a big part of our identities: I grew up confident in my intelligence and communication; Beth grew up confident in her looks. One more wonderful perspective to carry into my adulthood, to use in raising my own child – little things that are said can leave a lifetime impression on a child.

Neither of my parents were very tall: Dad was 5'8"; Mom was 5'4". It was no surprise, then, that Beth and I grew up short - neither of us is over 5'2" as adults now. Both dressed impeccably; and they dressed my sister and me that way as well. That's something that I have carried into my adult life. I take pride in how I look to this day. Our parents were very good looking when they were young, from the pictures I saw as a child. Both parents had beautiful brown, wavy hair. Both were rather small and good looking. Mom gained some weight, gradually, after having her two girls.

My mother was 100% French. Her parents were from Quebec. We think her grandparents were from France. I never found that out. I do know, however, that my aunt, my mother's older sister, didn't even speak English until she attended school. They all spoke French. I found this fascinating and alluring. I really wanted to speak French at a young age, like my mother's family had; but my mom only taught us a few words. My father was 50% French and 50% Irish. He had quite a temper at times.

We thought of it as his "Irish" temper; but I believe it was the combination of the French and Irish in him. I know I acquired that temper. There were many times Dad and I bumped heads because of our similar temperaments and strong wills.

Our parents were such incredible parents that, because of my health, they sacrificed their home and the life they knew in upstate New York to move us to Arizona when I was six years old. It was the medical belief of that time that people with asthma should move to a warm, dry climate. They sold everything they could, including my mother's prized possession - her baby grand piano. Mom loved playing the piano. She trained as a classical pianist. When she was in school she performed, with three other women, in the first radio broadcast of a classical piano concert. I have a beautiful picture that my mother had of the four women sitting at their pianos in long dresses. They were all quite elegant in the photo. My mother never bragged about her talent; but my father just beamed with pride when she played. She could play the most beautiful music, Chopin being our favorite. My mother sacrificed her piano and kept the swing for us. Well, of course, they couldn't put the piano on top of the car; but I know now what a huge sacrifice this was for her. They put everything they needed into a trailer, packing the car so that Beth and I could sleep in the back seat as if it were a bed for two.

They put our swing set on the top of the car (taken apart of course).

We were on our way to the great American Southwest. We moved to a new development, the farthest westside development in Phoenix at the time. It was a great neighborhood. Our house was modern, with big date palm trees in the center courtyard area of the front of the house. We had plenty of yard in which we could play, and often played at one of our many neighbors. Dad cemented our old swing set in the ground. I remember swinging on the swing for hours and hours. That was my quiet, alone time, my special time – to just feel like I was flying and dreaming about whatever I wanted.

I was not often nice to my little sister. When we wanted to play games together or play dress-up in some of Mom's things, we'd just get set up and I would say, "I don't want to play anymore."

I know I frustrated the heck out of Beth; and at times even did it on purpose. She was always the good child; I was the bad child, at least most of the time. I used to do so many things to make her angry. I'd lay in bed and make scary faces and noises just to scare her. I blew my nose in her hair one night, just to be mean.

My dad had a good job as an aircraft engineer. My parents put my sister and me in Catholic grade school. We were both honor students and enjoyed school. The class sizes were large – on the average 50 students in each class; but we received a lot of attention and a strong education. We also grew up knowing everyone in our classes, which stayed the same from grade to grade. The memory of those friendships has lasted my whole life.

My best girlfriend, Dawn, and I met in third grade and have been friends ever since. We are like sisters to this day.

We had to go to mass every morning before class started. We could all recite the Latin required in the masses, even if most times we had no clue what we were saying. I remember having a yearning of some kind while I was in church. I tried to determine what the yearning was. Was it a craving, like I was hungry? Was I thirsty? Was I feeling alone? It was a longing – something I remember very strongly. But it wasn't until I became an adult, in my mid-to-late twenties, that I figured out what this longing was about. It was my search for my soul, my connection with God, my spirituality. To piece these times together – the yearning or longing for something as a child in church and then knowing I was yearning for my soul connection to God when I was in my twenties – was a huge "aha" moment for me. Amazing how I could see this spiritual process and connect it with my childhood in church.

The nuns were quite a kick! They tried to instill the "fear of God" in us, sometimes just by talking loudly and firmly, or sometimes by cracking knuckles with a ruler if they felt a student wasn't paying attention. The principal, Sister Anne, was very strict and rather adamant about the fact that, as she told my parents one time, I couldn't possibly be having an asthma attack at school (as I did often) because I didn't have a fever. My parents met with her on that issue, just once, to let her know that she really didn't understand what asthma was, or how it could be exacerbated - and that was the end of that.

It was rather ironic that I had more asthma attacks in Phoenix than I had in New York – because there were dust storms often where we lived in Phoenix, a new development with a lot of vacant desert land, and I was allergic to dust. Phoenix was not the cure that my parents expected. But I survived. And, in fact, I outgrew my asthma when I turned thirteen.

While my dad had a good job, my parents couldn't afford Catholic high school, so my sister and I attended public high school. It was quite a shock to me, to be one of roughly 2,000 students – after growing up with more individual attention in my private school. Class sizes were even larger here. My Biology class had 200 students; we had lectures in the auditorium. This was quite an adjustment for me, being a number at a huge school. I hated it. I did what I could to make sure I still got good enough grades to make the honor roll; but I certainly didn't feel the 'school spirit'. I had so many great friends in Catholic grade school. In high school I had only one friend, Laura. We were the only two girls from our Catholic grade school who went to this public high school. I also felt very self-conscious as I had gained weight in puberty. I was not happy. I felt alone at this new school.

I still had my friends from Catholic grade school, especially my best friend Dawn; but I didn't get to see them as often as I wanted, sometimes just at church on Sundays. I started a Catholic Youth Organization (CYO) at the church, with about three or four teens in our church.

We got the organization set up, became board members and recruited teens to join. I pushed myself to be out there for this, forcing myself to lead when my self-confidence felt weak. I knew that I was doing what I needed to do to speak in front of others and build my confidence, despite not feeling good about my weight. I just instinctively felt I needed to force myself to build my confidence. I believe it affected my adult life greatly, making me step out of my comfort zone, teaching me to be confident in my speaking and leadership abilities.

A senior from one of the Catholic high schools, Brad, became the president of the CYO. I became the secretary. I was a sophomore and became very much infatuated with Brad. He was the captain of the football team at another Catholic high school he attended and was in the local paper often because of his team's success. I collected every article I could find that mentioned his name or, even better, had a picture of him in the article. I was sure I was in love. When he asked me to go to a basketball game with him, I was beside myself! This was my very first date, ever. My parents were ok with this date, even though I was still only a sophomore, because they knew his parents. They knew he was a 'nice young man'. I was just giddy about my date with Brad. He wanted me to sit next to him in the car when we drove off to go to the basketball game.

It turned out that Brad was playing me – the young girl who was so infatuated with him – and he made fun of the fact that my dad had met him at the door when he came to pick me up. I was mortified! It was all just a big game to him. When I overheard him say this to his team during the basketball game, I left and sat in a friend's car until they were ready to leave. I cried and cried. This was the first time I had really fallen for someone; and he made fun of me.

I didn't really forgive him for many years. I saw him a few times, a few years later – at his dad's funeral, and when I was out on a date with a friend of his in a club in Scottsdale - and I still looked at him with such dislike. Our mutual friend even said to me that Brad many times said he was sorry for what he had done to me; but Brad could tell I was not going to forgive him. He didn't apologize, even though I could tell by the look on his face that he was trying to. I was not nice, but, then again, I was so hurt. I should have forgiven him much earlier because the forgiveness would have been healing for me. I realize now, as an adult, that it was very unhealthy for me carrying that pain for any length of time, but I was at a very vulnerable age then.

Around the time I was going through my first heartbreak, my father's job was at risk. My father had worked for the same company for 17 years in Syracuse and Phoenix and he was concerned about layoffs. Then, after my sophomore year of high school, our parents told us we were moving to Seattle, Washington.

We were really upset and concerned about being away from our friends. And, of course, we heard that it always rained there! How could we survive?

We moved to a little city called Marysville, just north of where my dad worked for Boeing. It was, again, a shock to move to a very small city, a little tiny school one-quarter the size of the one I left in Phoenix; and it seemed like it rained all the time! I quickly developed some great friendships though; one lasting to this day, my dear friend Cheryl. I did well in school – made honor roll, joined organizations and felt good about my last two years of high school. I even started a Future Business Leaders of America (FBLA) with my business teacher – the first at that school. When I graduated from high school, I convinced my parents to let me move back to Phoenix, where I essentially grew up, to go to college. I just couldn't handle the rain or the small town. My intentions were to go to a community college and then transfer to ASU to get a law degree. I wanted to help people and solve legal issues. This was my desire; and I was told by a few of my teachers that I would be good at law. My best friend, Dawn, was going to college in Phoenix. I wanted to move back to 'the big city' and be on my own. And I did.

When I graduated from high school at eighteen, I thought I knew what I was doing, that I was a grown-up now.

I found a job right away at a bank operations center, on the graveyard shift. I also signed up for classes at the community college near where I lived with Dawn and her parents.

I started smoking cigarettes because I thought that would make me look more grown up. It was ridiculous to start smoking, because of my history of asthma. My parents smoked, so I thought it was ok. Little did I know how addicted I would become to cigarettes. I really didn't know how bad smoking was for my lungs; or I chose to ignore the messages at the time.

I also met Dawn's new friends, a group of young adults our age of different races who all belonged to a singing "moral rearmament" group called "Up with People". We had so much fun! We would sing in the sessions, then go out to eat together and just have a blast hanging out. We were a great group of teen adults. We also liked to shock people when we all hung out together in public. As a diverse group of black, white, and Asian young adults in the late 60's, early 70's, some people found it absolutely shocking that black and white young adults were dating! We sang about love and peace. We felt we had nothing to hide. We took pride in who we were and had no shame in our relationships. Race riots were occurring around the country; but we were flaunting our friendship. We felt like we needed to tell the world, in our singing and in our public display of friendship, that we were doing what was right – making a statement that we are all equal, no matter the color of our skin.

It was my own personal, social statement that no one had the right to tell me whom I could date. That included a black man.

One night I went to pick up my friend from "Up with People", Allen, at the gas station where he worked, in a mostly black part of town. I was told by Allen, "Absolutely do not get out of the car." There were riots occurring at times in that area of town; and, as a white woman, I could certainly be shot if I were to be seen there. I did heed that warning.

Allen became my boyfriend. He was a very handsome young black guy, and quite charming too. He was well-built and 5'11". He dressed impeccably, which also impressed me. He had a great sense of humor and could entertain a room full of people, when he had the opportunity. He was a senior in high school still. I loved going to his track meets and football games. He was a very good athlete.

I worked at the bank operations center at night, went to school during the day, and saw Allen whenever I could. This was usually during the late afternoons or evenings – before my graveyard shift. That didn't work very well: I barely left myself time to eat or sleep right and I got mononucleosis. I was given that diagnosis just a few days after Allen left town for a month to do a job, driving a large truck across the south, with a relative of his. I was flat on my back in bed for that entire month, sicker than I had ever been in my life.

Because I was so sick for so long, I lost my job and had to drop out of college. I had to start over.

As I finally recovered, I found another job, as a personal secretary to the owner of a small manufacturing company. I also felt good about my relationship with Allen. I did not tell anyone at the office that my boyfriend was black. The owner was an old-fashioned, Midwest man and would never have understood. To concentrate on my job and my love, I gave up going back to college for a while.

I wanted my parents to meet my boyfriend, so I talked Allen into flying with me to Seattle. My parents knew he was coming with me and that he was black; but I think of this situation as my "guess who's coming to dinner" moment in life. Allen was petrified to meet them. I assured him that my parents were very loving people who would accept him. And they did. They had raised us that all people were equal.

They did worry about how we would raise our children, if we were to have any, in a world that was not accepting of interracial marriage and mixed-race children, a true concern in the late 60's/early 70's. We understood; but we felt confident we could have mixed children and raise them to understand and accept their identities in a world that might not be so accepting. Because of my strong Catholic upbringing, I decided to practice the rhythm method as our form of birth control.

The Catholic church was adamantly against any form of birth control other than the rhythm method at that time. About a year into our relationship, I found out I was pregnant. This shouldn't have shocked us; but it did. Allen was panicked. I was too, although maybe not quite as much as he was. Allen's parents were ok with this news; they knew we were sleeping together. I was mostly worried about how I would possibly tell my parents back in Seattle.

This is when I had my first gut feeling that I would probably be raising our child by myself. I had no immediate evidence of that, just a strong gut feeling. Allen was not doing well with the idea of becoming a father or getting married. It turned out he started communicating with his ex-girlfriend from high school about this new situation. And he was suddenly torn between the two of us! This was a shock to me because I thought we were exclusive. I was devastated to hear that he was still seeing his ex-girlfriend, especially that he waited to tell me this when we were going to have a child. I told him I was not going to make him marry me or make him feel obligated to raise this child with me. I was devastated and felt alone and betrayed, and ashamed. I also knew I really let my parents down. I had dropped out of college and was now pregnant. I called my parents to tell them and said I wanted to come home. An unwed mother, going back home. Sad.

Because of my fears and shame, as a young Catholic woman, I bought an inexpensive gold band, put it on my left hand and told a big lie. My parents knew we were not married; but I didn't want their Catholic friends to know that. I was embarrassed for my parents and myself, so I lied and told everyone that we had gotten married in Phoenix but were separated. My parents were wonderful to me. They did not judge or condemn me. They were just upset for me that I made choices that were going to affect my life, and our child's, that could bring about added pain or difficulties.

CHAPTER 2

Our Child is Born

I realized that Allen might not be in our lives. So I started wondering: how did I choose the wrong mate? I believed that if you have a loving upbringing, with parents who set the example for you with a healthy, loving marriage, that you would just know how to make a wise choice in marriage. My parents were always kind and loving to each other. My father worshipped the ground my mother walked on and was always attentive to her needs. I was sure I had found the right mate until he couldn't decide between me and his old girlfriend.

Once I left Phoenix, Allen called me a lot at my parents' in Seattle. Every time he called, he said he wanted us to be together, to raise our child together. He convinced me that he loved me and wanted us to be a family. I moved back to Phoenix to have our baby, to be with him, and hoped that we would get married and be a happy family. My parents were concerned, but supportive of any choice I felt I needed to make. I flew back to Phoenix and moved in with Allen at his parents' house. I was five months pregnant at that time. I couldn't find a job, being obviously pregnant. I was small in stature with a big baby bump.

Allen had started a new desk job at the Highway Patrol, a job Dawn's father had helped him get. Allen's plan was to get admitted into the Phoenix police academy and become a full-time police officer.

My soon-to-be father-in-law had retired from his longtime job and would sit in the living room and talk all afternoon with me, while Allen and his mom were at work. Hal, Allen's dad, would drink his beer (it took me a while to realize that he was an alcoholic) and I would drink my Pepsi; and both of us would smoke cigarettes. I was oblivious to the fact that both of those things were terrible for our unborn baby. I enjoyed spending time with Hal. He was a sweetheart. Even as an alcoholic, he was always good natured and kind. Hal was a small man, weighing no more than 125 pounds and no taller than 5'4". He had been a good father to Allen and his brothers and sisters. Allen was embarrassed by his father's alcoholism. Hal would just pass out on the couch at the end of the night; and Allen would have to put his father to bed.

Our daughter, Mari Shea, was born two months premature. I'm sure now that it was because of my smoking. I didn't know at that time that smoking could cause premature births. I didn't realize, at first, that I was in labor. I didn't think I could possibly be since she wasn't due for another two months. I was scheduled to deliver Mari at the county hospital because we had no medical insurance and were not married; I didn't even have an assigned OB/Gyn. So I stayed home as long as I could. Allen's mom was an angel, staying awake with me many hours, rubbing my back and holding my hand through the labor pains. Allen was working much of that time. The labor started on Friday morning. Mari was finally born on Monday evening.

By Monday morning, I decided I couldn't take the labor pain any longer and had Dawn's mom, Mary, a RN, take me to the hospital. I labored all day until the nurses finally gave me something to slow down the contractions. Then they sent me home. I was ok until I had one long contraction all the way home. Allen had to rush home from his sister's house and go with Mary and me back to the hospital.

Mari weighed only 4lbs. 13 oz. Other than having under-developed lungs, Mari appeared healthy. She squeaked, rather than cried, like a little mouse. She was so beautiful, despite her little cone head (from the 4 days of labor). Mari really didn't look like I thought she would as a mixed black and white baby; she looked mostly white with only little, dark ringlets in her hair. I found out later that mixed children usually develop the tan complexion and nappy hair gradually, as they grow. Mari and I were in the hospital for three days, the norm for 1971.

Before Mari and I could come home from the hospital, Allen bought some new clothes for us to dress her in. Because she was premature, there was no time for anyone to give us a baby shower. The clothes were for newborns; but they overwhelmed Mari's tiny little body. We had to find baby doll clothes to put on her until she could grow into the newborn outfits. I was terribly crushed that Allen didn't bring me flowers. I had labored for four days and delivered our beautiful daughter and received no recognition. I was quite hurt over that, which added to my depression.

No one explained why I felt like crying all the time while I was in the hospital. They didn't mention that post-partum depression could be the common answer.

We had to take turns waking Mari up every two hours to get her to eat, just to keep her alive. Premature babies love to sleep and would not wake up on their own to eat, the hospital staff told us before we took Mari home. Mari would not breast feed as well, so we had to put her on formula. It was stressful; but we both did well keeping Mari alive and healthy. I was surprised at how well Allen managed to help with Mari and catch some sleep before going to work each day.

One day I decided I just had to get out of the house and we needed more diapers. Allen and I put Mari in her baby car seat (which was smaller than normal and not like the car seats of today) and brought her into the store to buy what we needed. I put a little, light blanket over Mari, so the sun wouldn't be in her eyes. I didn't take the blanket off her in the store. We put the car seat, with Mari in it, into the grocery cart and proceeded to do our shopping. People stopped us to ask, "Is there really a baby in there?" Sitting in her tiny car seat, only a few weeks old, Mari looked like she was only about 6 inches tall. She was really 19" long at birth; but sitting in this little car seat made her look incredibly small. I, of course, was proud to show her off to everyone who asked. Allen was not quite as thrilled.

"How could you let total strangers breathe all over our baby?" he said. I just laughed. The people didn't really breathe all over our baby.

We married when Mari was 7 months old. Allen had asked me to marry him a few months after Mari was born. I felt Allen wanted us to be a family. We ended up divorcing when our daughter was two years old. Little did I know then that this was the beginning of a rough road for our daughter, the beginning of her life without a father. I raised our daughter by myself, without any personal (and very little financial) help, other than from my parents. My parents had moved back to Arizona to be near their new granddaughter. Raising Mari by myself was partly my choice, but also because my ex-husband very quickly married his ex- girlfriend.

Allen had been seeing his old girlfriend while he and I were married, and she became pregnant with his child. In fact, his mother knew that Allen had been cheating on me for a year and didn't tell me. I was really upset with her initially until she explained that she didn't know how to tell me. She had tried to get Allen to "man up" and tell me himself. He didn't. One of his older sisters told me. I was devastated and furious when I found this out. I quickly dumped Allen's clothes and things out onto the front sidewalk of our apartment. Allen had been accepted into the Phoenix police academy and became a patrol officer; and he wanted his girlfriend, rather than his wife, to attend his graduation from the academy.

He was seeing his ex-girlfriend for a year; and I didn't know about it. When my ex remarried, he became a father again, and again, and had no time for his first child. I was baffled how a parent could abandon their first child simply because they have other children. A parent will always be the parent, for the life of that child.

We quickly learned that Mari had medical issues. Like me, she was born with asthma. She was sick more than she was well for the first two years of her life, with constant upper respiratory infections. I don't think Allen knew how sick Mari was because we were separated. He did not ask how she was doing; and I was so angry about his betrayal I chose not to speak to him. He was so preoccupied with his pregnant girlfriend as well. When she was two, just shortly after Allen and I had divorced, Mari became exceptionally ill, with a temperature of 104+, and I was panicked! After trying to keep Mari's temperature down with baby aspirin that weekend, I decided to go to my parent's house and have my mom help me with Mari until I could get her to the pediatrician on Monday. As soon as I got to their house, I asked my sister, who was still living with my parents at the time, to hold Mari while I ran to a drug store to get some more baby aspirin for her fever. I was gone about 15-20 minutes.

When I came back my mother said, in a very calm voice, that we had better take Mari to the hospital. She was starting to have a seizure.

OUR CHILD IS BORN

If it weren't for my mother and my sister being there for us I think I would have literally lost it. My parents had just moved into their house and didn't have a phone yet. We loaded Mari into the back seat of the car in Beth's arms; I sat in the front passenger seat; and my mom proceeded to back the car out of the driveway. Beth said that Mari was in full seizure by this time. I jumped out of the car and ran into the neighbor's house without knocking and grabbed their phone. I could barely dial the numbers. The neighbor could tell I was absolutely panicked and luckily was able to take over and make the 911 call for me. The ambulance attendants had me sit in the front with the driver and would not allow me in the back with Mari. The driver drove VERY FAST. I knew that the paramedics were trying to save my daughter's life as best they could. When I heard the person in the back talking to the hospital to report ahead, he said some code and then I heard "possible code arrest". I started going hysterical, probably screaming like the siren of the ambulance. I was sure my baby was going to die. I was absolutely panicked that we wouldn't get to the hospital before my daughter completely arrested. I remember telling the people in the hospital, who were taking Mari's gurney to a room, that she had been sick for a couple days, and that "I only gave her baby aspirin." I was sure that I had done something wrong and had caused this! I was so afraid my baby was going to die.

I called Allen right away from the hospital. He drove to the hospital quickly. Once the doctors had stopped the seizure and given her medication to keep it from reoccurring for a bit, they recommended that we take her to the hospital where her pediatrician practiced. They felt it would be best to have him take over her care. Allen drove Mari and me, very quickly, to the bigger hospital in Phoenix where her pediatrician could see her. We felt we could get her there safely without requesting another ambulance.

Mari was in the hospital for five days. It was an intense five days, with the fever always ready to rise. My baby had more tests done in those few days than most adults have in a lifetime; but they could not find what caused the high fever. They kept her packed in ice for many of those days, just to keep her fever from rising. It was so scary to see my child like this. She was so lethargic and helpless. I stayed with her day and night. I could not leave my baby to feel alone and abandoned in her hospital crib at night. I remembered what is was like for me at age two being left in the hospital alone at night without my parents. Luckily the hospital staff allowed me to stay.

She was diagnosed with an upper respiratory infection and was on IV antibiotics; still the fever would not break. When the doctors took Mari out of the ice packs and felt it was safe to take her home because her fever had subsided, I took her home. My mother came over to help me take care of her.

My mom could tell that I was a mess. I had never been so worried about my baby, especially when no one could tell me what caused her fever. My mom decided that afternoon to give Mari a bath since she really hadn't had one while she was in the hospital. As soon as she put Mari in the warm water of the tub, Mari broke out in a rash. She had the chickenpox! I felt so relieved because we figured out that Mari had the chickenpox virus in her, along with the respiratory infection, and the warm bath water had allowed the pox to finally pop out on her skin. Amazing! Even the doctors couldn't figure out she had the chickenpox virus in her. Thank God for my mother!

Mari was doing much better and really didn't have any further signs of respiratory infections. Her pediatrician had said to me that he expected she would outgrow her asthma by the time she was two and a half. I thought he was insane! How could he possibly predict that? But it appeared he was right.

Shortly after this medical scare, when Mari was three, I was offered an opportunity to move across the country with the company I was working for in Phoenix. It was merging with a much larger company in Philadelphia. I was very fortunate to be asked by the corporate office to move to Philly, as there were only five of us in the entire Phoenix office asked to move. The last time I had lived in the northeast part of the country had been when I was just a few years older than Mari.

I felt this move was good for me as I could heal and build my confidence again by taking on a new job, with more responsibility and increase in salary, in a new city. I was trying to pull myself together with all that had happened since Mari was born. I thought this would also be a new life for Mari and me, even though she was only three years old. My gut feeling was telling me that Mari would be without her father, perhaps forever, as Allen didn't care that I was taking our daughter out of the state. He was remarried and had a new daughter. He had seen Mari only once since she had been in the hospital.

I decided to take the job and move to Philadelphia. I chose to live in New Jersey and commute on the highspeed line to Philadelphia each day. The company paid for all the moving expenses, including the trip for me to fly Mari to Seattle to stay with my parents so they could take care of her while I got our place settled in Philly. Mari really didn't understand the move even though I explained it to her. She was just excited to be with me, and my parents. This was great for Mari to have time alone with my parents. My parents were able to spoil their first and only grandchild as much as they wanted, without my objection. Mari spent about a month with them. I was able to get settled into my apartment and start my new job, then bring Mari to her new home in New Jersey. My first few days of work were spent right in downtown Philadelphia until I was able to move into my new apartment and commute, via the high-speed line, from New Jersey to Philly every day.

OUR CHILD IS BORN

It was a great adventure. At least I thought so at first. On the first day going to work in Philadelphia, the five of us from Phoenix walked many blocks to the office from our hotel. It was a very hot, humid day. I didn't have any idea how far it was from our hotel to our office. Both were downtown. Our boss, who was one of the five who had moved from Phoenix with us, knew Philadelphia very well. He had grown up there. He was entertained by my bold, but naïve, decision to walk.

As we were laughing and joking about our walk in the heat, a city bus hit a man who crossed in front of it! The bus had not been traveling fast; but the man looked hurt and did not get up. I had never seen anyone get hit; and I was really upset. I wanted to stop and help him. Our boss stopped me from running over to help the man and explained that the bus driver would take care of him and call an ambulance. Wow! He explained that this happened all the time in the city, at least in this city. I was in shock. On my first day going to work in this big city, I saw someone get hit by a bus!

I felt very fortunate to find a babysitter through the leasing office in my apartment complex before I brought Mari to our new home in New Jersey. Nancy came recommended by others in the complex, which was nice to find someone others trusted. Over many months, there were nights we had to work overnight to meet our deadlines, especially when there were new computer equipment glitches.

Nancy was always willing to keep Mari when these work emergencies occurred. I felt the babysitter was a life-saver. But then Mari started acting strange. One night when I went to put her in the bathtub before putting her to bed, Mari screamed hysterically about getting into the water. She was absolutely petrified. She screamed and cried and said, "No Mommy. I don't want to go in the water!" She just stiffened her little body and refused to go in the tub. She had never done anything like this before. She was never afraid of the water. I was shocked to see her act like this. I talked with Mari to calm her down and find out how she could suddenly be so afraid of the water. Thank God she could speak so well for a three-year-old. I found out that Nancy had physically abused my daughter. Mari had wet her pants a couple times when she was outside playing. Mari said, "Nancy was mad at me for wetting my pants outside, Mommy." I freaked out but tried to remain calm and asked Mari, "Why did you wet your pants honey? Couldn't you just go inside Nancy's house and go to the bathroom?" Mari said she didn't know. But as we talked a little more, I concluded that she was just having too much fun outside on the playground, playing with the little boy Nancy took care of with Mari every day. Mari told me that Nancy turned on the shower, with cold water running, and made her get in that shower with her clothes on, as punishment. She traumatized Mari! She had never been in a shower in her life, and certainly not in cold water.

Mari was obviously petrified that she was in trouble with me and was afraid I would turn the cold water on her in the bathtub. I could only imagine how confused and hurt Mari was when Nancy did this to her. I'm sure she thought she did something so wrong to have Nancy hurt her like this. A child can't comprehend this kind of behavior from an adult in charge. I'm sure she thought she was a bad person. This hurt me to the core.

Nancy never said a single word about the incident when I picked Mari up that day. She hadn't even told me about Mari ever wetting her pants. I was livid! I explained to Mari that it wasn't right that she didn't go in the house to go to the bathroom when she was at Nancy's; but I also explained that what Nancy did to scare her with the water was very wrong. I took my time explaining to Mari that she was not a bad girl.

The next morning when I took Mari to Nancy's before I went to work, I told Nancy that she was NEVER to do that to my child again! I didn't look for another babysitter because I was sure Nancy would never hurt my child again. I believed in disciplining my child, but certainly not by traumatizing her in any way. I never felt Nancy had a right to hit my child. She should have let me know about Mari wetting her pants and I would have taken care of the situation. Mari listened to me and was always a good child.

I thought that I had things back to normal with Nancy caring for Mari. Meanwhile, my job was getting to be more and more stressful.

The company was making more demands of me and not living up to the promises they made to me when I took that job nearly a year before. And I felt I was neglecting Mari when I had to work late. I gave my two-week notice and planned to move, at my own expense, back to Phoenix. I had a new job offer before I left Philadelphia with the help of one of my coworkers from our old office in Phoenix.

Then one evening before I was about to leave the job, I went to get Mari ready for her bath when I discovered that she had bruises all over her arms and back. I screamed. I'm sure I scared her. I kept looking at her little body in disbelief and horror. Once I calmed down a little, I asked Mari how this happened. She said, "Nancy hit me with the brush." I was shocked and angry. I instantly saw red! I asked Mari, "You mean Nancy hit you on your body with a brush?" I wanted to think I was not hearing this right. It couldn't be possible! I asked Mari, "What happened? Why did she hit you with the brush?" Mari said, "I wet my pants again, Mommy." I know I went hysterical. How could anyone hurt this beautiful little three-year-old like this? Over wetting her pants? My God!

I had so many emotions. Mari then told me that Nancy had also thrown her little kitten on Mari when she was taking a nap, waking her up with the cat's claws scratching her and scaring the daylights out of her. This woman was insane! How could she possibly do something, or any of these things, to an innocent child?

My first thought was to call the police. I knew this was child abuse. But I also realized that I would have to stay in New Jersey until we went to court for this and I could see Nancy go to jail. I had made all the arrangements to move back to Phoenix. We were to leave in less than a week. I was torn. I really wanted to go to Nancy's and kill her for what she had done to my child!

I explained to Mari, one more time, that what Nancy did to her was a very bad thing. I think that Mari thought she was a bad girl and was afraid to tell me the things Nancy had done to her – thinking she was in trouble. I told Mari that wetting her pants was something we would work on; but what Nancy did to her was not right. I told Mari, "You're not a bad girl! What Nancy did to you was very wrong. You won't have to stay at her house anymore." I then gave Mari her bath and put her to bed, gave her a huge hug and left the room to cry and decide my next step. I needed to calm down a little. I then called a close friend and asked him to come over. When he came over, I called a friend I worked with who lived in the same apartment complex and asked her if she could come over to watch Mari for a few minutes.

I went, with my male friend, to Nancy's house to talk to her. I know I had my friend with me to keep me from hurting Nancy the way she had hurt my child. I told Nancy she would never see Mari again. I said, with as much constraint as I could possibly bolster, "You should be beaten for this! How could you possibly hurt an innocent child with a brush? You are an evil person and you should go to jail for this!"

Nancy said nothing. I really wanted to hurt Nancy the way she had hurt my child, but I knew I could not afford to be charged with assault. I then said, "If it weren't for the fact that I am moving back to Phoenix, I would call the police and have your ass put in jail right now! But I would need to stay here to go to court and make sure you are punished for this; and I can't stay. So consider yourself lucky!"

To this day I am tormented by this decision. Why didn't I fight for Mari and have this woman locked up? Maybe I could have prevented Nancy from hurting another child. My beautiful, little child had been traumatized by this woman!

Mari and I moved back to Phoenix, into my sister's apartment, until I could find a new apartment of our own. This worked out well. My sister, Beth, had moved back to Phoenix when my parents did, when Mari was two. However, my parents went back to Seattle shortly after that, while my sister stayed in Phoenix. Beth had a new boyfriend, Mark; and the three of us adults, and Mari, somehow managed to live in this old, very Spanish-style, apartment not too far from one of the city's famous parks. It was quite cozy. We made this one-bedroom apartment work well for us. Mark and Beth turned the dining room into their bedroom, and Mari and I took the bedroom and slept together there.

I had a great job working for a small database service bureau as an assistant to the manager. I learned even more about computer operations and was able to run the IBM mainframe at times, with the help of the computer operator. It was a good job.

OUR CHILD IS BORN

I was soon able to afford my own place, an old house I rented right across the yard from my sister's apartment. I was thrilled to have my own space; Mari and I got to have our own bedrooms again. We loved our home, the neighborhood, and still lived close to my sister. Not surprising though, Allen, Mari's dad, was still nowhere to be seen, even though he knew we were back. He still lived in Phoenix but was too busy with his new wife and kids.

I found a daycare/preschool for Mari that a neighbor had recommended. I checked out the daycare, which was a little bit out of the way in getting to work; but it was well worth the drive. An amazing, older couple ran this daycare. They were like grandparents to the kids. They had a little swimming pool at the daycare and taught all the little kids how to swim. This was Mari's first experience in learning to swim and she loved it. No more fear of the water. The daycare couple bought a new reading program to teach the kids how to read. The program taught a unique version of phonics that was tailored for preschool children. It was awesome! This reading program was groundbreaking at the time. Mari loved it. Things were going so well for us; Mari and I were both very happy and content with our lives. My job was going good and Mari was doing exceptionally well in preschool.

The daycare owners had someone come into the daycare to test the children's vision. Mari was extremely farsighted and needed very strong glasses to be able to read.

Discovering she needed strong glasses at the age of four was a lifesaver for Mari. I'm sure her vision had been affected by her five-day, high fever and seizures she had at the age of two. I read that high fevers can do some permanent damage to children, many times affecting vision or hearing. Once Mari got her new glasses, she could read as well as any child in first or second grade. I had to tell my little girl that she was still beautiful, even though her glasses were so thick and strong. She was so darned cute with her little afro, tiny four-year-old body, and very strong glasses. She looked very smart and she was.

One day at work a salesman, selling radio commercial time, came in to speak to the manager of the data service bureau. My desk was in the lobby. I had to speak to him, taking his business card and information, then announce him to my boss, Jay. The salesman was so good looking he nearly took my breath away. He was tall and thin and quite professional. I hadn't seen a man in a suit look so professional since I had worked in Philly. I buzzed Jay on the intercom to tell him I wanted to speak to him about this salesman, then I went into his office. I had a great rapport with my boss. He was like a father to me; and I could speak to him openly. I said to Jay, "There's a really good-looking man in the lobby who would like to schedule a meeting with you about buying commercial advertising time. Could you please make him come back and wait when he's here for his appointment?" Jay just laughed and said, "Sure, why not?"

He looked at his calendar and came up with a date. I was thrilled. I kept my cool, stayed professional and announced to the waiting salesman the date Jay would be able to meet with him. He agreed. And, the salesman (believe it or not I still can't remember his name) flirted with me and left.

When the Kirk Douglas look-alike salesman came back for his scheduled appointment, I announced to Jay that "Kirk" was here for his appointment. Jay had no one in his office; he played along with me to keep this good-looking guy waiting a while. Kirk and I had quite the conversation. By the end of the meeting, in which Jay never committed to buying commercial time, Kirk had asked me out. I was so excited. I was elated that my plan worked, and I had a date with one of the most attractive men I'd seen in my life. I felt pretty confident in my looks as well – I was proud of my long auburn-brown hair and I had slimmed down after having Mari. I kept my cool, even though I felt like dancing around the office. I hadn't dated much since Allen. I had been too busy working and managing my life with Mari.

So now I just one hiccup - to figure out who I could get to babysit Mari that night. I rarely needed a sitter since, after Mari's awful experience with Nancy, I was worried about whom I could trust. My sister and her now-husband had moved to California a few months earlier; my parents were in Seattle again; and my ex-husband was too busy to see his daughter since he had a new family. Yes, I believe Allen saw Mari one time since we had moved back to Phoenix. One time.

Luckily, I still had a great relationship with Allen's family. His mom took my side in the divorce and saw Mari often. She had known that Allen was cheating on me while we were married; and she didn't like it. She had been there for me during the pregnancy, during the divorce and I loved her like another mom. So Mom was glad to have Mari spend the night with her and her two youngest children while I went out on this date with Kirk.

Kirk picked me up for a night of dinner and a concert. We had a good dinner with somewhat good conversation. I could tell he was quite egotistical, that the evening would consist of him talking about himself. He certainly had no real interest in asking about me. I was determined not to feed his ego. I was just that way. When the check came for the dinner we had just enjoyed, Kirk pulled out his wallet and proclaimed that he had forgotten his credit card. I was livid. After all the bragging, I couldn't believe it. What a game. I paid for dinner. This date was not what I had expected. We went to the concert, Boz Scaggs; and it was wonderful. I had always liked Boz and was thrilled to see him in concert. Kirk had prepaid for the concert tickets, so, thank God, he didn't ask me to pay for that too. When Kirk drove me home, he expected to come in. I told him, "only for a minute" and I meant it. He was pretty upset when I let him stay only a few minutes and told him it was time for him to leave. He drove off with tires screeching. Oh well...

I was able to deflate his ego though. He dropped in our office a few days after our date. He didn't have an appointment with Jay. He wanted to try, one more time, to convince Jay to buy radio advertising with him. I went into Jay's office and told him Kirk was back to see him. We worked out a plan to have Kirk meet with him for a minute and ask him to come back later for another scheduled appointment. When Kirk left his office, Jay told me that Kirk bragged about how I was so infatuated with him, that I had even asked him in after our date. I went ballistic! This was a déjà vu of my very first date in high school with Brad. I could not believe that this egotistical jerk was twisting our date to sound like I was so interested in him. It was quite the opposite. When Kirk came back for his appointment with Jay, Jay kept him waiting for a long time. This gave me time to ask Kirk to go outside with me and take a walk. I absolutely blasted him for talking about our date to my boss. I also said, "I don't know who you think you are, but you're not a great catch! You're egotistical, self-centered and you made me pay for dinner. I would never date you again." I also added, "And Jay has no intention of buying commercial time with you." He was speechless at first. I'm sure he had never had a woman talk to him that way. He apologized for what he did and said he didn't realize he appeared to be so egotistical. He was quite grateful for someone telling him this – or so he said. And I felt damned good!

One day Jay told me that a friend of his mentioned a condo for sale in Fountain Hills, east of Scottsdale. It was a unique opportunity in that the owner just wanted someone to assume the loan of this condo. It was an amazing deal.I took one look at it and bought it. It was affordable and was the first home I bought on my own. The only downside was it was way out in the desert, about 45 minutes away from my office and Mari's preschool. It was also a little scary driving at night. I had a new car, but I still wondered what I would do if my car broke down. How could I be sure Mari and I would be safe out there on the dark and desolate road to Fountain Hills? It was a great investment, and a beautiful little two-bedroom, two-bath condo. But I felt very alone out there. Mari and I started staying with my ex mother-in-law during the week and going to the condo on the weekends. Mom had divorced my ex father-in-law sometime around the time Allen and I had divorced. She was so giving and loving. She was struggling to make ends meet but she always welcomed us in to her home. I had a good relationship with Allen's family, including his sisters. I just didn't have a good relationship with Allen, however, and neither did Mari any longer. He never stopped by to see his mom, or Mari, when we stayed there during the week.

Shortly after I moved into the condo in Fountain Hills, I met a man, Chris, who came into our office to have some work done for the company for which he worked. He was nice; and the more we talked, the more we became friends.

We found we both loved jazz. We dated for a while and, while on these dates, I usually had Mari stay with Mom or one of Allen's sisters because I was still concerned about who took care of Mari.

One night I invited Chris to go with me to a Johnny Mercer concert for the Fountain Hills homeowners. I took Mari to Allen's oldest sister's house. Barbara and her husband had a son, Clark, who was approximately 12 at the time. I had known Allen's sister, her husband and son for years. They were happy to have Mari stay with them for the night.

I had not actually heard of Mercer at the time I invited Chris; but I soon learned that Mercer was very well known. The concert was wonderful. We walked around the grounds after the concert. The stars were out in the open, clear, dark Arizona sky; and the fountain shot to the sky, it seemed, like it was reaching for the stars. I picked up Mari at Barbara's the next day. It was good to have Mari back with me, on our way to Fountain Hills for the weekend.

I don't know to this day how Mari came to tell me, how she said it, or how she had the courage to say what had happened to her when she spent the night at her aunt and uncle's house that night. I only know it was a very, very long time after that night, almost six years, when she finally told me. Mari was around 10 years old when she told me; she was four when she had stayed that night with them and her cousin was 12.

She said Clark had raped her that night and two or three other times when she stayed with her aunt and uncle! She didn't use the word rape; but she clearly described to me what he did to her. It was rape. But Mari did not tell me then. I'm not even sure what prompted her to tell me so many years later. I just know that I never had any idea that this had occurred! How could I have not known this? And how did Clark's parents not know this? Mari never complained about any pain. She didn't even act like anything was wrong! As her mother, how could this have happened; and I never had a clue? By the time I discovered what had happened to Mari at age four, we had already moved away to the Seattle area.

I called Allen's mom in rage. Her reaction was ridiculously calm. She said she was not surprised because she heard from another family member that Clark had tried to rape his own mother one night when she was drunk; but Clark's father stopped him. This was the darkest, sickest story I ever heard! Why hadn't she told me about this when she knew I was taking Mari to stay with them? I was furious with the whole family for keeping this a dark secret that would scar my daughter for life! Why did no one really stop this rapist? How could they allow their son to continue to live a life of rape and molestation without putting him in counseling, a psychiatric facility or, better yet, putting him in prison? I think Clark's parents were both alcoholics and may have never known that Clark had done this to Mari; but they knew what kind of a sick person he was.

OUR CHILD IS BORN

Because it had happened to Mari so many years before I even knew about it, I felt defeated. I thought I would have no way to file any criminal charges against this guy. I had to let it go. But every time I thought about this, I was sick about it. I felt betrayed by my in-laws, especially when I found out that many of them knew about Clark. This was now the second time in Mari's life I had left her with someone I truly trusted – and they abused my child! I had to face the fact that not only did people abuse my child, I had no way to do anything about these heinous crimes. I felt I could not have justice for the trauma my daughter had experienced.

Mari seemed relieved when she told me about Clark. I explained to her that she had done nothing wrong, I could never be mad at her for what Clark had done to her - something so terribly wrong. I told her he should pay for what he did to her but because I did not know that he had done this to her at the time it happened, I could not do anything about it now. I told her I was so sorry that she got hurt by some people that I thought I could trust. I was devastated for her. I hugged her and cried for her. I knew my baby would be scarred for life by this.

I felt that Mari was so relieved to get this out in the open with me, and she knew it was in no way her fault that this horrific abuse had occurred, so I didn't think to put her into counseling. I was about to learn years later that probably wasn't a wise decision on my part.

CHAPTER 3

Many Changes

While I was unaware of the terrible events going on with my child at age four, the great data processing service bureau job that I loved so much was about to end. The company suddenly had new ownership and gave notice they would be closing the office within a month. This was just after I bought my new condo. I panicked at first, then put my condo up for sale, thinking it would sell quickly. The real estate market was good.

However, I discovered there was a huge problem. There was a legal dispute over water rights between the Native American tribe who owned the land adjacent to Fountain Hills and the Fountain Hills homeowners. Everyone in Fountain Hills panicked that they would suddenly have no water. Many people on my block put their homes up for sale. Because potential buyers were spooked, the sale of my home didn't go as I planned.

We moved back to Seattle, with a real estate agent handling the sale for me. It finally sold when I allowed someone to assume my mortgage. I found out after I sold my condo that the water rights dispute was resolved. If I had kept the condo and just made the ridiculously low payments myself, or had my parents help me with the payments until I got back on my feet, we would have had a perfect place to stay when we went to visit friends in Phoenix.

Or we could have rented it out. I sure wished I had kept it, but I didn't. I found out a few years later that those condos were selling for many, many times what I had paid for mine. Fountain Hills became a very exclusive, expensive area in which to live.

Just before moving back to the Seattle area, I decided to go to a priest, a family friend, for advice. I was at a turning point in my life, reflecting on what I had done - what I was feeling unhappy about in my life - and I wanted some help. My Catholic upbringing had entrenched a strong fiber of guilt in me – feeling guilty that I had dropped out of college, married too young and divorced so quickly.

I never felt guilty about having our daughter – just that I had married someone who abandoned his own child when he and I divorced. I knew I could handle the responsibilities of raising my daughter by myself, but I was still very emotionally raw from all that had occurred in my young adult life. I had even gone to a counselor for a while. I was doing some soul searching and needed some advice. I needed to feel closer to God and have Him help me release some of my pain and guilt. I found myself pulling away from the Catholic church after I got pregnant with Mari, especially when the rhythm method didn't work for us and I started questioning, "Is the Catholic church going to help me raise this child now?" I wasn't angry at God, just the church. I asked the priest, "How will I feel God in me?" "I feel", I said, "that God will come to me through my mind."

The priest said, "Then that's the way God will come to you." He didn't really give me the answers I expected. I wanted more advice from the priest. I wanted him to disagree with what I said and say, "Oh, but this is the way he'll come to you." But he didn't.

That was the beginning of my inward, and outward, search for God. I couldn't get my fill of spiritual and metaphysical books. This was my way of searching for God - through books. And it was much cheaper than paying for a therapist. I was on my own spiritual journey.

Mari and I moved to the little city of Marysville, where my parents were living again and where I had attended my last two years of high school in Washington. My parents really liked that city. It was small, quiet; and they had a lot of good friends. I still didn't like it so much; it still looked the same as it did when I went to high school there. My parents loved having us stay with them until I found a new job and a place for us to live. Mari was still their only grandchild, so they lavished her with lots of love and attention. It's amazing how grandparents can be so very different from what they were as your parents. My mother was especially attentive to Mari. I guess I was a little jealous that she was much more fun and in the moment with Mari than she was with me when I was that age. I don't remember my mom playing with my sister and me like she was with Mari. I was certainly happy to see how much they loved their granddaughter though. Mari needed that love and attention.

I found a job quickly, near my parent's home; and my Mom walked Mari to her new school. She was starting kindergarten. I had mixed feelings about Mari starting grade school. My baby was no longer a baby!

I found a three-bedroom apartment in Everett, just about fifteen minutes away from my parent's house, that I could rent with a girlfriend of mine from high school. We were off, Mari and I, to share this nice new apartment with Cheryl. It was fun. Mari developed new friendships with the neighborhood kids, and her new school friends. We felt settled and happy.

Sometime after moving into that apartment, I received a call from my ex mother-in-law, Mom, saying that her oldest son, Allen's brother, Harold, had been shot and was not expected to live. It had occurred at his apartment that he was sharing with his best friend, also a friend of mine. But the details of how it happened were very sketchy. I wanted to get down to Phoenix so badly; but I couldn't afford to go. It bothered me tremendously that I couldn't be there for Mom. And I loved my brother-in-law dearly. He was a wonderful man. Harold passed away a few days after I received the call. I was devastated. Also, I think this is when Mari became afraid of dying, something that would haunt her for a long time. She asked me lots of questions about her Uncle Harold; and I could sense the concept of death was new to her and worried her. I couldn't understand how anyone could have done that to him.

And I heard from the family that the police in Tempe basically didn't investigate his death very seriously, saying, "well that's one less 'ni----' we have to deal with!" I was beyond shocked!

This was 1975. Allen was a Phoenix policeman at the time, so he went to the Tempe police department to question their investigation. He got nowhere. Tempe may not have had many black people living there but it was a big university city, so it should have been more tolerant. I was furious. Harold was an upstanding young man, citizen and an EMT, not some flaky criminal.

Mari was doing great in school and with her friends. When she was eight she wanted to take dance lessons. I signed her up for lessons at a local dance studio. She was quite good. I was sure this was because her mom and dad were good dancers when we were a couple. Mari was still tiny and petite, with a rather large afro and her thick glasses. Still my little nerd, and beautiful. Mari was fantastic in every type of dance: jazz, ballet and tap. Mari especially loved jazz. She was totally distraught, however, when she wasn't picked to perform in some recitals – as were some of the instructor's favorites. Mari gave up on the dance classes all together then. She decided that if she wasn't going to be considered the best, she didn't want to do it anymore.

For Halloween that year, I dressed Mari up as a Christmas present. We had a big cardboard box and lots of Christmas paper to wrap around the box.

MANY CHANGES

I cut holes in the box, on each side, for Mari's arms. Then I put a great big bow on her head. She looked so cute. I still have pictures of her in that costume. Cheryl, my mom and I walked around the neighborhood with Mari that Halloween night. Mari was having a little problem seeing where she was going since the box stuck out so far from her body. She was doing just great until she walked up a driveway that had sand-filled paper bags with candles in them lined all the way up to the front door of the house. Mari slipped walking to the door, fell and couldn't get up. She was like a little turtle on her back. I ran like crazy to help her up. I could just see my daughter going up in flames! She was fine. I remember the homeowners being upset though, not because Mari could have been hurt, but because their candles got rearranged! Some people can be so uncaring. It was a Halloween no one forgot.

We lived harmoniously in that apartment for a couple years. Ironically Cheryl didn't like kids and I didn't like cats. Cheryl had three cats and I had Mari. But we all got along great. I even learned to like her cats; and Cheryl, of course, really loved Mari. I had a boyfriend for a little while. Bad choice for me; but he was good to Mari. He wasn't working at the time we dated, so he became a housekeeper for us and nanny to Mari.

However, Cheryl, our roommate, was not happy with me having him there and I certainly didn't blame her. She just felt uncomfortable around him. She bought a home in the north side of the city and moved out. When I ended the relationship with the boyfriend, I took in another roommate, Ray. I had met Ray through some mutual friends. It was just a roommate situation. I was not interested in him. It worked out well, for a while anyway. Then a couple of very intense incidents occurred.

A girlfriend I worked with had a little boy Mari's age. His name was Jamie and he was a beautiful mixed black and white child, like Mari. They played together very well. Each time my girlfriend and her husband wanted all of us to go out dancing together, we got a babysitter to take care of the kids at my friends' house. I evaluated the babysitter very carefully to make sure our children would be well cared for, based on our past babysitting experience. Mari and Jamie became good friends.

One day Jamie was playing outside in his neighborhood and decided to cross the street while pushing his little truck. He was bent over pushing the truck and a car coming over the hill did not see Jamie until it was too late. The car struck Jamie and he was severely injured. He was hospitalized for months. He was lucky he survived. But he had a rough recovery for years, learning how to walk and speak all over again.

This devastated Mari, and all of us. It scared me that this could happen to a beautiful, innocent child who was just not being careful crossing the street. What if Mari had been playing with Jamie that day? It taught me to stress to Mari how important it was to always be careful when playing outside and to pay attention to her surroundings. I also comforted her – she was so distraught – and let her know that Jamie would be ok. And he was. It just took a very long time. It was so sad to see him struggling to get back to the happy little boy he once was. And it affected Mari more than I realized at the time. I think Mari, at the very young age of ten, had her second exposure to the fact that anyone, no matter how young, can die or come close to death. I also think she hated to see her friend struggle. She was sad for him.

Sometime after that, on a beautiful, crisp Thanksgiving weekend, Ray and I decided to take a day trip up one of the North Cascades passes, one with beautiful mountain views with steep drop offs on one side. We took my mother, Mari and Ray's daughter, Hallie, who was staying with us for the holiday and was a couple years younger than Mari. Ray had just bought a new two-door, luxury car; and he wanted to take it for a little drive. It was starting to snow as we were headed east. We turned around once we got to the top of the pass so that we could get home while it was still light out.

Ray wanted me to drive home, just so I could get used to driving it in case I ever needed to use it. I didn't like the idea of driving it; but he trusted me. As we headed home on the pass, the snow got thicker and icier. Ray and the girls were in the back seat, taking naps. I could see the snow plow two cars ahead of me, so I felt the road was clear. When the snow plow pulled over to let cars go past it, the car in front of us continued to go extremely slow. I decided to pass him. Not smart. Just as I got the car next to his rear wheels, our car spun out. The car circled around and around I don't know how many times; I lost count. I just remember seeing the white mountain on one side and the steep drop-off on the other side! Luckily our car hit the snow-covered mountain and slid sideways into the ditch. When we hit the mountain, my mother and I both hit our heads on the windshield and broke it. My mother hit her mouth on the dash board and put her teeth through the bottom of her mouth and broke her wrist. I hit the steering wheel with my mouth and broke my front tooth. I was knocked out for a while. Ray told me later he tried to get me to open my door to let him out to make sure I didn't damage the under-side of the car - which could possibly catch fire! When I came to and opened the door, I looked over at my mom and realized she was sitting in a pool of blood. There was blood all over her face. My adrenaline was flowing as I jumped out of the car and grabbed some snow to put on my mom's mouth to stop the bleeding. The girls woke up and saw the blood.

Then Mari was afraid and started crying when she looked at her grandma. Thank God they were asleep during the accident and had not been hurt.

We were pulled out of the ditch by a couple of guys with a tow truck who happened to be driving up and down the pass, pulling people out of the ditches all day long. The car was fine other than the front bumper. We drove home, which was at least another hour, and rushed the girls to a neighbor's house so that I could take my mom to the hospital. She needed forty-plus stitches in her mouth and a cast on her wrist; but she was ok. I knew she was in pain; but she never complained. She was just like that. I had called my dad from the hospital and he met us there. I went to the dentist on the next Monday and needed some dental work but was fine.

I felt guilty about causing this accident. My God! I could have killed us! I was just impatient and should have gone slower in the pass; but that was my first experience driving in snow and ice. We were so lucky. I had no idea, till many years later, how much this traumatized Mari. She told me later how she was afraid her mom and grandma were going to die then, adding to her phobia of death.

Ray and I decided to buy a home together, in the north side of the city. The parents of the injured boy Jamie were getting a very ugly divorce and selling their house. I thought this would be a good investment for me. However, I should have followed my gut feelings on this – not to buy the house with this man.

My intuition was telling me that the energy in the house, and the energy between Ray and me, was not good. We hadn't even signed the papers on the house when Ray started drinking hard alcohol. I hadn't seen him drink like this. He could drink beer and be pleasant; but when he drank hard liquor he turned into a very ugly person. As I thought it was still a good investment, I signed the papers and moved in. It wasn't even a month and we were fighting like cats and dogs, because of Ray's ugly temperament when he drank. This was my second exposure to an alcoholic. My ex father-in-law had been the first and was very pleasant-natured when drinking. Ray was very confrontive and argumentative. His confrontations brought out an anger in me I had never experienced before and didn't like at all. I knew we needed to get away from this man. I felt he could hurt me, or I could hurt him; and I knew I would never allow a man to hurt Mari or me.

Ray left one weekend to go out of town. He had his own friends and I had mine. I took this opportunity and called a friend to help me move everything I owned out of the house that weekend. I did not want an argument or confrontation with Ray. I just knew we needed to leave right away. I didn't care about losing my investment in the house. The safety of my daughter and myself was my number one priority. Luckily Mari never experienced the arguments between Ray and me; she was usually outside playing or the arguments were late at night.

I didn't tell Ray where we moved to: a beautiful townhouse apartment, back in our old neighborhood.

Once we were settled into this great apartment, I felt safe about Mari's life and where we were. Mari had lots of good, happy years as she grew up in schools in Everett, from first grade through middle school. She had many good friends that she played with in the neighborhood.

Mari was really growing up. She was twelve and blossoming into a beautiful young lady; but she still had to wear her glasses and wasn't very happy about that. She felt like a little nerd and wasn't comfortable with her looks at this age. She was doing well in school and had many friends. I was very proud of who she had become. But she also developed a little snotty attitude at times preteen-girl, nasty, talking-back kind of stuff. We certainly had some discussions about her attitude. She was grounded at times.

Mari expressed a desire to see her dad once and a while. Since he was not keeping in touch with Mari, I felt I needed to make the contact and I would call him. I flew her down to Phoenix to stay with her dad and his new family a few summers during her last few years of grade school. She developed a good relationship with her half-sister while she was there. I'm not sure she ever felt like she had a good relationship with her dad. I guess it was better to see him once and a while, even though their contact would drift into nothingness unless I initiated it. I truly wanted Mari to have a healthy relationship with her dad. I felt that was very important for her. She needed to feel that her father loved her.

Mari excelled in grade school. She was in many advanced classes, a grade or two ahead of her actual grade in school. In middle school, however, she had a 6th grade teacher who was adamant about her belief that "no child should be in any advanced classes before going into high school." The principal of the school agreed with this teacher. That ruined Mari's interest in school as she became bored with regular level classes. I looked at the possibilities that would allow Mari to go at her own pace in school. I had her tested at a private school, a Baptist Academy. This school had a very progressive curriculum in which students studied and tested at their own pace. If Mari went to that school, beginning in 7th grade, we calculated that she would finish high school at the age of 16, based on her test results. I was a little concerned about what Mari would do when she graduated from high school at that age. I thought she might be too young and immature to go to college at that age.

My father also had an absolute fit about Mari going to that school. He did not want his Catholic granddaughter going to a Baptist school! I conceded. I didn't want to fight over this issue. My dad was so Catholic, there was no way to convince him that going to a Baptist academy would not hurt Mari in any way. But I doubted that was the right decision for Mari. I had Mari continue in public middle school.

I had been divorced for many years and was ready to date again. One unforgettable date had a spiritual, emotional and physical effect on my being. I was walking down the street in downtown Seattle one evening on this first date. The experience I had was so overwhelming that to this day I don't remember the man. I just remember the experience. We were walking in the rain and suddenly I stopped, put my hands up and let the rain pour down on me as I felt it washing me, healing me, loving me. It was the first time I felt God physically, emotionally and spiritually. I remember crying and crying. I'm sure the date thought I was nuts, and I never saw him again. Because of that experience, I realized God can come to me in many ways – in my mind, in my heart, in my body. I just need to be open to Him. It made me think of my conversation years before with the priest, how I explained to him that I wanted to feel God in me.

One night a girlfriend of mine, whose daughter was a friend of Mari's, asked me to go with her to a nice club in Seattle, near Elliott Bay. It wasn't that I wanted to drink, or even intended to meet a man, I just loved to dance. I hadn't danced in quite a long time. My girlfriend's neighbor, Deb, babysat her two kids and Mari. She was a great babysitter and took no guff from any of the kids. She became a good friend of ours from that time on.

I met a man named Evan that night. We were quite attracted to each other and we danced together till the club closed that night. Evan, also black, was strikingly good looking, tall and well-built. He was in the Navy, stationed in Bremerton. He took the ferry over to Seattle whenever he was on weekend leave. We spent more and more time together. Mari got to know him very well.

She and Evan would go roller skating as often as they could when he visited on weekends. They both loved to skate and were very good at it. They could glide, skating backwards, better than most people could going forward. I would watch. I was terrible at skating and was afraid of falling. I hadn't skated since I was a little girl, skating on our sidewalks in my little metal skates that fit over my shoes, those vintage frames that tightened on with a skate key. Anyway, Mari and Evan had no fears and could skate in a skating rink for hours and hours.

The more time we spent together, I could picture us becoming a family. I could picture Evan becoming a good father for Mari. I had known for years that Mari needed a father in her life. I fixed meals for us, envisioning the three of us eating together all the time. Mari made her teenage comments at times about how she felt that I was trying to pretend we were like "The Brady Bunch" or something. This was her teenage objection to a need I had for acting like a family. At times Mari felt like I was trying to "pass off" some of my discipline responsibilities to Evan. And I was. Mari had no real father figure growing up, so I thought this relationship could be a good parent/child relationship for her.

She would have none of it. Also, Mari had been used to it being just her and I for so many years.

This was a time when Mari was also showing her sassy, snotty, argumentative attitude, fighting me on almost everything I told her to do. I was nearly at wits end trying to get her to do as she was told. I caught her one day in her bedroom with a couple of her girlfriends smoking. When I opened the bedroom door, the girls all threw the cigarettes out her second-story bedroom window. They realized they were all caught in the act. I was so furious, mainly because she was sneaking cigarettes when she had lectured me for years about how I should quit smoking. I was so angry I couldn't speak. I told her girlfriends that they needed to go home. When they left, I lectured Mari, with some yelling involved, about how furious I was that she had lied to me, and how sanctimonious she had been about smoking. She never smoked again – at least at that young age – around me anyway. I'm sure she did it at one girlfriend's house because that girl's mother was so lenient.

I found out about how lenient she was, many years later from Mari, because Mari then admitted that she had smoked pot at this girl's house and she didn't like how paranoid it made her feel.

I took Mari to a counselor that specialized in teen behavior because I had read about "tough love" and felt that was the way I needed to handle her behavior. I went to that counseling appointment with Mari's chores list I had prepared. When the counselor tried to tell me that I needed to "share some of the chores with Mari and 'negotiate' this list with her,

I said to Mari, "It's time to leave." I explained to the counselor that I was the parent in the house and I would not "negotiate" the chores I expected Mari to do. I didn't have a huge list for Mari; and I always kept a clean house. I was determined that Mari would do things to help, like keep her room, bathroom and the kitchen clean after she ate. These were not unreasonable requests. And I won this argument with Mari. I said, "I'm the mom; and if you want to live here you will do the simple chores I ask you to do. There's no negotiating."

Mari wanted to spend the summer in Texas with Allen's mom, "to get away from us," she said. I agreed it was a good idea. Mari was also going through a tough identity time in her early teen years, having a racial conflict between the black and white in her. Because there were few black kids in her school, and even fewer mixed kids, she said she didn't like the black part of her – and felt guilty about it. I could see it was really bothering her. And, also, Mari had no black relative to relate to. I explained that she was a "beautiful mix of the black and white in her" and would learn to love who she is. She was a beautiful girl; but she wasn't owning it yet. I agreed she should spend some time with her black grandmother in Texas, thinking she'd feel more comfortable about her black identity. Mari stayed with her grandmother for a month that summer and turned thirteen while she was there. She came back with much more confidence in who she was and felt more resolved about both sides of her identity.

She had a lot of fun as well, just hanging out with her grandma, Aunt Regina and Uncle Fritz.

Evan and I were together as much as we could be, every chance he was on leave. However, the time came for Evan to leave the Navy and Bremerton. I don't think I was really prepared for this or what I would soon find out. He went back to Chicago, where he had grown up, to finish college and get a nursing degree, even though he had been working on an electronics engineering degree in the Navy. I really felt he could be a lifetime student. He promised he would come back to Washington soon so that we could be together.

Then I found out that he was still married! He had been married the whole time we were together. I sent him a card and his wife found it. She called me and said they were married and had an eight-year-old son. His explanation for his lack of honesty was that he had been separated from his wife for years. I told him to never call or write again. I was devastated. For all her complaining, I was sure that Mari was attached to Evan; and this breakup hurt her as well. He persisted on calling and writing me. I told him that he would have to prove to me that he was divorced; and I had no intention of carrying on a long-distance relationship, so he'd have to move back with this proof before I'd consider continuing anything. Evan ended up coming back, within a year, with all the proven documents, and we married. However, it only lasted six months, and I had one more bad marriage. I had a strong gut feeling that it wasn't right to marry him and chose to ignore it.

Our relationship had started out with his dishonesty. But I didn't listen to my instincts. I thought I had really taken enough time to know myself in the twelve-plus years I had been single. I thought I knew how to make wise choices when it came to men, at least by that time anyway. Not so.

In fact, my mother started saying to me, "For someone who is so smart, I don't know how you can be so stupid when it comes to men." She said this one final time at a dinner party that I had gone to with my parents, at a friend's home. I heard it too many times from my mom; and I was so furious that she said this in front of friends at dinner. I walked out of that dinner party and didn't speak to her for days. That hurt incredibly. But the truth hurts sometimes. I know she was so sorry she said it, especially that time, because my dad called me to say I needed to forgive my mom. Mom was devastated that she had hurt me like that. We talked it out and were fine after that. But I certainly knew I would never say anything like that to my daughter.

Evan moved back to Chicago. I waited eleven years before I filed for divorce. I just couldn't handle another relationship going bad, so I was determined to stay out of relationships - by staying married. Mari seemed to be ok with my short marriage, like she really knew all along that it wouldn't work out either. Kids can see some things, and see into some adults, clearer than adults can sometimes.

CHAPTER 4

Friends

Despite Mari being bored in middle school, she liked public high school. She had many friends of both genders. She was popular. She also didn't need her big, thick glasses anymore; I had her vision tested to make sure. She suddenly morphed into this beautiful new swan. She was a tiny, very strikingly beautiful teenager with a beautiful, naturally tan complexion. She had an exotic look, people said. Her striking look attracted many boys. However, many of the girls became jealous of the attention she got from the boys. They were quite mean and cruel. We learned that teenage girls can be little 'mean girls' and bullies. I had not experienced that kind of meanness when I was Mari's age.

Mari was quite upset about the jealousy and meanness she was experiencing. She had never experienced this in her life. She had been called some names, like the 'N' word, a few times; but had never experienced this bullying and nasty gossip before. I raised Mari just as I had been raised, to be honest, kind and loving. She was also incredibly loyal to her friends. Now those 'friends' were turning against her. She had a very hard time concentrating on her studies.

Mari loved dancing, since her dance classes she'd taken when she was younger. She and I used to dance in our living room together many times over the years. There was a dance club, in downtown Everett, just for young teens under the age of eighteen. Mari was fourteen. It was well supervised and had excellent security; and I knew her friends that went there as well. Her best friend, Lynn, picked her up and brought her home when they went to the club. They had a lot of fun and were good about making it back by curfew. One time, however, they came home a little late. Mari and Lynn walked in the front door and I was shocked to see Mari looked a mess, like she had been in a fight. She was scratched up and had been crying. They explained that one of the girls, who was supposed to be one of Mari's friends, had punched Mari in the face, knocking her down in the parking lot. Mari was not a fighter. This, again, had been about some girls being jealous over Mari getting attention from some boys. I called the police. Mari didn't want me to because she was afraid of the retaliation that could occur, not only from this girl but also from the group of girls that hung around her. But I thought this situation with the jealous girls was totally out of control! The policeman came to our home and took a report.

The father of the girl who hit Mari called one evening shortly after this fight. I was sure he was going to rant about how it was "just a little misunderstanding" among teenage girls.

FRIENDS

He shocked me by saying, "I'm a Seattle policeman and my daughter knows better than to act like that. She should pay the consequences for what she did!" I explained that Mari didn't want to press any charges now; but we hoped his daughter had learned her lesson. That girl later apologized to Mari.

I could tell Mari was stressed about this whole ugly "mean girl" issue. She was so above that pettiness. She didn't care about any of the boys that these girls claimed as their boyfriends. She just wanted away from this mess. She was struggling. She really wanted out of that school. I moved Mari to another high school in the city, hoping that she wouldn't have to deal with the petty, mean distractions of jealous girls and could get on with her classes.

I'd like to say that the rest of Mari's time in high school was good; but it wasn't. I knew that Mari liked a young boy, Dante, who went to a different high school. I met him; and I met his parents, who were very nice people. Mari even had a good relationship with Dante's older sister. Dante appeared to be a nice kid. He was only fifteen and Mari was not quite that old yet. I was very careful about the time she would spend with him. It turned out that Mari was seeing Dante much more often than I knew. She would say that she was seeing a girlfriend and really be sneaking off to see Dante.

One morning Mari came into my bedroom saying that she didn't feel well and ached all over. She didn't look well. She had a fever and was burning up! I figured she had the flu.

I told Mari that I needed to take her to the doctor right away because her fever was so high. I remembered her fever ordeal when she was two and didn't want to ever see her have a seizure again. Mari started crying and saying, "No, Mom, I can't go to the doctor." This made no sense to me. "What are you talking about honey? You have to go. You are really sick; and that fever could be serious." Mari kept crying and crying. I said, "Mari what is wrong?" She finally admitted to me that she was pregnant and didn't want me to know. She intended to have Dante's sister help her. How, I'm not sure. My fifteen-year-old daughter was pregnant. I was shocked. I took her to the hospital that morning. They confirmed she was pregnant and she also had a very serious case of Strep throat that had settled in her joints and muscles. If I hadn't taken Mari in that day, she could have died from the Strep infection.

I knew that Mari's pregnancy meant that she had been seeing Dante much more than she had admitted to me. I was devasted for my child. It was so incredibly sad to think that she had made this choice in search of male love and attention. I had read somewhere that if a person is molested as a child, that child could become a promiscuous adult. There was no doubt that this situation, no matter what her decision would be to carry this child or not, would affect her for the rest of her life. I had no idea what I could do about this. At that time, I just wanted to help Mari make it through this. She was, after all, still a child herself.

FRIENDS

Mari's 'boyfriend', Dante, was no help, consolation or even a friend when Mari found out she was pregnant. He abandoned her. Dante's sister had been the person Mari could count on, taking her to the store to get a home pregnancy test. But, because Mari was just fifteen, there was nothing any one of them could do without my consent. I went to Dante's parents to talk with them about this situation. They were supportive of whatever we decided to do. I explained to Mari that, even though this was totally against what I was brought up to believe as a Catholic, I felt she needed to have an abortion. I just knew this would be too much for Mari to handle, trying to raise a baby at the age of 16. I think Mari understood what I was saying and could visualize how difficult it would be for her to try to raise a child at that young age. She had the abortion, based on my urging. I was right by her side through the abortion and recuperation time at home. I could tell she was depressed. I did not realize until much later in Mari's life that this pregnancy, abandonment by someone she felt she loved, and the abortion left a serious scar on her psyche. One more scar, a huge scar.

As if it wasn't painful enough to have gone through this situation, Mari told a girlfriend at school she trusted about her pregnancy and abortion. This girl betrayed her trust and told many of the friends she knew. This absolutely devastated Mari! Now many of the 'mean girls' were talking about Mari like she was trash. One guy friend of Mari's came to Mari's defense. But the damage had been done. I knew she was on the edge.

She had been betrayed by so many people in her young life, people she had trusted to take care of her, to be her friend and she was barely hanging on by a thread. I knew that Mari could not take one more betrayal, one more hateful gossip situation in her life, or she would break. I took Mari to a psychiatrist for the first time. He was a good psychiatrist, as good as anyone could possibly be for her at that time in her life.

Mari wanted to leave that school, just hoping she wouldn't have to deal with the harassment from the mean girls. I had already switched her from one high school to another, and back to the original school. I told her there was no way she could just quit school. I saw that Mari could not continue in either high school, so I decided to take Mari out of high school and put her directly into the local community college, where she could get her GED and continue without missing a step - taking college courses there. It worked. She was finally in her element. She was now back to doing well, moving at her accelerated pace and dealing with adult-like students. She no longer had to deal with petty distractions.

She loved it in college. And she was only 16. I felt if I had stuck to my guns and put her in that Baptist Academy like I had wanted to when she was in middle school, maybe she could have avoided all the high school drama and done just fine at 16 – in college. Instead we took a long, ugly route to get her there.

Now that Mari was in college, I felt that she was doing well away from the stress and pettiness of her high school days. She was happy. She was back to her old funny, cheery self like I had not seen since she was in grade school. She took some basic required classes and an art class. Mari was very good at drawing. She had a natural talent and instinct about art. She decided she would go for a graphic design degree. She didn't like it, though, when the teacher explained that as a graphic designer she would have to redo her designs to meet the desires of the clients. She was not happy about the idea of having to redo her work when she was happy with what she had created. She said she couldn't be creative on a deadline. I encouraged her to consider becoming an artist, an architect, or maybe an interior designer. She considered all this.

While Mari was in college, and now seventeen, she met the stepson of a dear friend of mine. John was a couple years older than Mari, although Mari seemed older than her years. They started dating and became inseparable. They were a beautiful couple together. I could tell that Mari and John were falling in love and were happy. John had a good job and treated Mari like a princess. I was sure they would be together for many years.

Years earlier, I attended a series of seminars called "The Excellence Series" in Seattle. It was a life-changing experience for me. Now I wanted Mari to take the courses, even though the age requirement was 18. Mari was still 17.

I knew what my life benefits were from this program, so I was sure they would benefit Mari. I thought they would help her deal with some of the demons from her past and help her heal. The concepts of the seminar series were that everyone is accountable for their own actions and no one is a victim. It had the attendees view some painful events in their lives, taught them ways to forgive themselves and others for their past difficult experiences, then gave them practices to help them visualize their future lives.

We got permission for Mari to attend the first seminar, "The Pursuit of Excellence." I went to Mari's first seminar graduation. I could see that it had affected her very emotionally, as it did everyone who had attended the seminar. So, I was not surprised to see her so overwhelmed. But it turned out that attending the seminar was a terrible idea for Mari. It took a few months for the pain from this seminar to have a serious effect on her. I never saw it coming.

John and Mari were still dating. Mari was still going to college and doing well. Things seemed to be going super for Mari. One night, John called me, very upset, saying that he didn't know what to do. He was trying to keep Mari from killing herself. She was in his bathroom trying to commit suicide. I told him to take her out of the bathroom, by holding her in any way he could, and take her to the closest hospital. I don't remember thinking at that time. I was in shock. I met them at the hospital. Mari was obviously very distressed, like I had never seen her before.

It was clear that if John had not been there for her, she could have succeeded in killing herself. John was devastated as well. He thought everything was going so well with them. He couldn't understand how Mari could want to end her life. The doctor decided to put Mari in an in-patient psychiatric ward at the hospital for two weeks.

I took some days off from work so that I could visit Mari at the hospital. I couldn't stay with my baby, though, like I had when she was in the hospital at two years old. Mari was on anti-depressants and they monitored her carefully to see how the drugs would affect her. She was also in private psychiatric sessions, and classes, to help her through her depression. When I decided to go back to work, thinking that work would help take my mind off the seriousness of my daughter's situation, I found that no one was talking to me - even my friends who knew what had happened with Mari. I'm sure they just didn't know what to say; maybe they were afraid of opening the pain, so they said nothing. When someone finally did come up to ask me how Mari was doing, and how I was doing, I absolutely lost it.

I had not cried the whole time Mari was in the hospital; but I cried like I had never cried before. My sobbing was uncontrollable. I knew Mari was in excruciating emotional pain; and I was too. I felt like my child had a terminal illness and there was nothing I could do to help her. I was sure I was watching her die.

I realized that I needed compassion at that moment at work. I had never experienced knowing, at a specific moment of pain, how I needed something so badly from someone else. It was quite an awakening, just moments after becoming aware of my need for compassion, that the question came to me: "How could I expect compassion from anyone if I don't know how to give it?" I realized that I had never really been a compassionate person myself. That one person showing me compassion opened the gate to my need to show compassion. And the person I needed to show compassion, more than anyone in my life, was my daughter Mari!

The person who talked to me that day, took me to her home that afternoon away from everyone and everything at work. She let me talk and cry. I needed that so much. Then she told me her story. I had no idea what she had gone through, years before, when she lost a child. I never forgot that woman and her kindness. We worked together a few years later. She was an inspiration to me.

CHAPTER 5

What to do ?

While Mari was in the hospital, I was wrought with guilt and wondered, "What could I do for my suffering child?"

I felt so responsible for her devastation. I had let her down as a parent, left her with people in her past who had abused her, and then put her in a crash-course seminar that ripped open her emotional pain. I felt terrible. I knew that the seminar had brought all the raw, painful experiences of her past back up to the surface, yet I didn't know what to do for her other than take her to any and every psychiatrist I felt could help her. I also called her father. I thought he should know. I thought that maybe if he came up to see her, which he did, it could help heal Mari's father abandonment pain. This was the first time she had seen her dad in years. I had sent her a few times when she was younger to see her dad and stay with him and his new family, in Phoenix, for a couple weeks during the summer.

Allen came to Washington to see Mari while she was in the hospital. Mari was very happy to see him. I'm sure she felt like he was worried about her and truly loved her. He stayed for a few days, made her many promises to stay in touch, and left. I wanted to yell at him about how his unfulfilled promises to stay in touch could, and had, hurt her; but I didn't.

He had neglected her for so many years and only stayed in touch with her when I initiated it. Allen had also tried to go for long periods without paying the court-determined child support, causing me to confront him with his back-child support payments often. I tried to never speak poorly of Mari's father around her; but she knew of the conflict I had with him paying child support. Mari would say to me at times, "He can't even help you raise me. He doesn't even feel I'm worth anything!" I told her many times that he loved her; but sometimes I doubted that he really did. He certainly didn't show it. I calmly let him know that her fragile psyche really needed to have her father stay in her life.

Mari dropped out of college because of her hospitalization and out-patient therapy. I went to the dean of education at the college to see how we could save the credits she had accumulated. The dean was a good friend of my father. He was very helpful and concerned for Mari.

John still visited Mari. He was obviously very worried about her. Mari, however, told John that she could not see him anymore. This devastated John. Mari gave up that wonderful, loving relationship with the man who saved her life. To this day, I'm not quite sure why. I'm not even sure if she knows why she did that. I can only guess that she felt she was unworthy of his love and could not put him through her pain. But I know she loved him. I was terribly sad for Mari that she made this decision.

WHAT TO DO?

Mari attempted suicide three more times in following years, going through much in-patient and out-patient therapy. There were so many times she would call me, crying and talking about "how she couldn't take it anymore." I felt so helpless. She saw a therapist, took medication for depression, and yet was still talking like she didn't want to live. I could only listen to her and feel her pain. Depression is such an insidious disease.

I truly had no idea how to help her. How could I help her erase what had happened to her? No matter what I said or did for her, I never felt like she believed in herself. She had lost all hope and trust in herself and others. I do know, though, that I tried to keep our lives as normal as I could possibly could. I felt like she was so fragile, always on the edge of wanting to escape this life of hers. If we had good days, months even, I felt like we were on the right path. Sometimes she seemed happy, for a while anyway. Most of the time I felt she needed to be near me, so that I could see that she was ok.

CHAPTER 6

Back on Track

Once Mari seemed to stabilize with medication, she and I moved to North Seattle. Mari wanted to work in Seattle and go to North Seattle Community College. She was starting over in school, still unsure of what her major might be. She was determined, though, to at least get her college requirements for a degree out of the way. I think she realized this was one way she could feel good about herself.

Mari also worked three part-time jobs while going to school, which impressed the heck out of me. One of the jobs she had was working in the pharmacy of a big chain drug store. She worked as a B Tech, handing the prescriptions to the customers and ringing up their purchases. One of the pharmacists told Mari one day, "You know, if you take the pharmacy tech program at the college, and you graduate and become certified, you can double your salary." That's just what she did. The program was intense; but she passed, and was certified, with flying colors. I don't know how she did it. She was going to school, focusing on this program especially, and still working her three part-time jobs. And she was getting a 3.8 GPA. I was so impressed with Mari, so proud of her. She became a licensed Pharmacy A Tech and made much better money.

Mari's best friend from high school, Lynn, had moved back to the area to go to college.

Lynn had a beautiful new baby and they both came to live with Mari and me in our two-bedroom apartment in Seattle. I now had roommates. Mari, Lynn and baby Daniel had one bedroom, and I had the other. It worked out well for all of us. Lynn became my 'other daughter' when the girls were in high school and her son was my new 'grandson'. The girls were focused on their grades; but they also had a great group of friends who kept them socially alive as well. It seemed like Mari was really doing well again.

Within this group of friends, Mari and Lynn both met new boyfriends. Lynn became involved with a nice guy, Dustin. We all liked Dustin a lot. Over time, Lynn and Dustin moved further south of Seattle and then married. He became a great dad to Lynn's son Daniel. Lynn and Dustin didn't have a lot of money; but they were happy. Mari became involved with a great guy, Max. Because Lynn had moved out, I moved into another apartment complex and Mari and Max moved in with me, as roommates, until they could find their own place. It was a beautiful apartment, with a beautiful view of the east side of North Seattle. It had a unique two-floor layout, which I loved, with the main floor consisting of the kitchen, dining room and living room, and the bedrooms downstairs. We loved it there and were quite comfortable living together. I gave Mari and Max their privacy. I wondered if they would get married; but I never pressed the issue with them.

I was still working in Everett, north of Seattle.

The commute wasn't bad; the traffic to and from work was going in the opposite direction. However, when Mari and Max found their own apartment, I decided to move back to Everett. I moved into a small, but very cute, one-bedroom apartment very near my office. It was a huge apartment complex; but I lived in a quiet area. I loved it there. And this was my first time living alone.

I didn't see Mari and Max or Lynn, Dustin or Daniel very often. I had Daniel stay with me one weekend when he was just a little more than two years old. I had so much fun with him. He was my first 'grandchild' and I was in heaven. Everything he said and did was so darned cute. And he was a very good child. I was his only nearby 'grandma' because Lynn's mom lived on the other side of the state.

The adults were busy living their own lives. I had to request time to see them. They seemed so grown up, even though Mari was only nineteen. She was working in pharmacy full-time. Max worked in the cable industry. They were doing well and seemed to be happy. For the first time in a long time, I felt that I didn't need to worry about Mari's depression. She seemed okay. I breathed a sigh of relief.

I had a good job with a major telecommunications company that I had worked for many years. I had transferred to different departments over the years and developed a good knowledge of the industry. My last job with that company was in a call center.

I had some great responsibilities within that department, including as an assistant to the project manager setting up that call center. I loved it. I also became the assistant to the department manager once the center was up and running. This woman motivated everyone who worked in that department. She was incredibly demanding; but she was also inspiring. She was also very understanding when I unexpectedly needed to take some time off from work when my mom became very ill.

My mother had diabetes and COPD but had managed these two diseases well over many years. Suddenly, just a few days before Thanksgiving, my father told my sister, Beth, and me that he thought Mom had the flu and they wouldn't be having dinner at their house. It became apparent soon, however, that it wasn't the flu that Mom had. She was diagnosed with congestive heart failure. That was Thanksgiving. My mom passed away on Christmas morning – one month from the date she became ill. It was extremely difficult for all of us: my dad, Beth and her family, and Mari and me. My sister had remarried and had a daughter now, Allison, and a stepson, James. We took turns being by Mom's bed, for days, waiting for the day we had to let her go. We also had incredible help and support from Hospice before Mom died.

Mari was the first and only grandchild for years and they'd had a very close relationship. She had spent so much time with my mom and dad when she was little. Mari was devastated again. She adored her grandmother.

We were also sure my father would be like those people you hear about where the spouse, who has lost their very long-time love, dies within a year. My father adored my mother. They were married over 45 years when my mother died. But my dad surprised us all and lived another 15 years.

Max had been there for Mari during my mom's illness and death. I was so glad Mari had Max there for her emotionally. He knew how much Mari's grandparents meant to her. They seemed to be doing well. They had their own apartment, good jobs and appeared to be very happy. They got engaged. They didn't make a big deal about it. I thought they should have; but they seemed very excited about it when they told me.

Not long after their engagement, Mari and Max broke up, again. This was not their first breakup, I discovered. Their relationship was much more volatile than I knew at the time. This breakup, along with the death of my mom, brought Mari to her third suicide attempt. Her second attempt, not as serious as this one, was treated by a psychiatrist referred to her by her doctor. This suicide attempt, however, brought her to another in-patient facility. I could see now that Mari could not handle any breakup or loss. She was so incredibly fragile and so vulnerable to loss. She just couldn't handle losing one more person! I could see she was in so much pain again. I could only hug my adult child one more time and trust the doctors, hopefully, could lead her out of her of her depression again. And she had also been traumatized again.

I found out from Mari that during this breakup with Max, she ran into an old guy friend of hers, someone she really liked and trusted as a good friend. She not only valued his friendship, but also loved his mom and had a great relationship with her. He invited her over to his house and they got close, too close. Mari explained to me that he tried to rape her. He just wouldn't take "no" for an answer. She was devastated and felt betrayed, one more time, by someone she thought she could trust. I could not understand how one person could have so many devastating things like this happen in her life. I was afraid she might crack and never come back to life.

Shortly after my mom passed away, while concerned about Mari and her mental health, I became a supervisor in the call center. I had a lot on my plate. I had worked in that department for a couple years. I realized that the building was very old, built in the 1970's, and had poor air flow and circulation for the number of employees in the building. I found out that 1970's constructed buildings were built very air-tight. That was the way, it was perceived at that time, to save energy. Many of the on-line reps were getting ill, coughing like crazy. I couldn't stop coughing, which brought back my asthma. I took a lot of time off and went to many doctors. When I figured the problem was in the building itself, I brought this up to the managers. I realized that I would never be able to get management to fix this.

I knew I couldn't get anyone to change this situation and I left the company. Without another job.

When I had left my job, without another one ready to jump into, I had to take some money out of my savings to live on. Maybe not so smart; but I felt relieved about leaving that company. They were starting to retaliate against me as I brought the 'sick building' issues up. They were questioning my integrity. I had never experienced that before. When I gave my notice to leave the company, I had an instant 'weight taken off my shoulders' feeling. And I was finally getting my health back.

My dad still lived in Marysville, not wanting to sell his house after Mom died, so I moved in with him for a short time until I found a job and a new apartment. I think my dad enjoyed having someone around since Mom had only been gone a couple years. My dad and I were quite alike, with strong French/Irish tempers; and I was worried that it could be difficult living together. But it wasn't. We got along super; and I was not at home much because of a very long work commute every day when I started a new job.

Mari was twenty and living in her own apartment now, very independent. She dressed impeccably and looked like a model. In fact, she was approached by someone who suggested she get into modeling. I paid for her portfolio; but modeling jobs never appeared. She was told she was much too short to be a model. We got some beautiful pictures out of the deal.

She worked as a pharmacy tech at hospitals, doing very well. She had recovered from her last suicide attempt and had a better relationship with Max, even though they were off and on. I was still very worried about her though. We had talks on the phone where she sounded upset about Max. I just never knew when she would be devastated again and feel suicidal. Because of her past, as her mom, I just couldn't feel confident that she was happy, even when things appeared to be going well in her life.

CHAPTER 7

A Big Birthday

I hosted a big 21st birthday for Mari at a beautiful restaurant and bar on Lake Union in Seattle. It was a big deal for her, and for me. She was thriving after some very harrowing ordeals in her short life. She was such a beautiful, grown-up woman now. I was in awe of her. Mari seemed happy. She and Max were in love again. Her close friends were there. It was a great celebration. I also decided to give Mari a wonderful, surprise birthday present – a one-day cruise out on Lake Washington to see the Seafair Hydro races. It was an all-day event. I drove Mari, Max and myself to the cruise terminal at Lake Union. The boat took off at 10 am. The boat was cruising slowly and enjoyably to Lake Washington. It was a gorgeous day with blue skies and sun. The cruise staff started serving alcohol at 10 am when the ship left the dock.

Many people were completely intoxicated by noon, when the time trials were starting for the races. Mari was one of those intoxicated people. Even though Mari had a few drinks at her 21st birthday party, I had never seen her drink like this before. I don't think she knew how little she could drink, especially since she was a very tiny woman. The cruise ship staff also decided to allow people to get soaked with hoses on the top deck of the ship because it was so hot that day. This was in August; and it gets hot in Seattle at that time of year.

At least hot for the Northwest. But the drinking and the wet, slippery feet going up and down the cruise ship was an accident waiting to happen. That accident happened to Mari.

Mari had gone downstairs to go to the bathroom, slipped on the floor and hit her head on the sink, then on the floor when she fell! I didn't know this until I saw Max carrying her upstairs to the main deck to lay her down. A nurse on the cruise looked at Mari and said, "I'm sure she has a concussion!"

The cruise ship contacted the Coast Guard to send a boat to come and get us, take us to a medical triage spot, and then on to a local hospital, in Kirkland, via ambulance. Yes, Mari had a concussion. We were instructed on what to look for in Mari, over the next few days. But we also now had no car. I had to call my sister and brother-in-law and ask them to come and pick us up and drive us to my car on Lake Union. It was a long drive for them; but they did it, thank heavens. I'm sure Mari never forgot the disaster of a 21st birthday she had, even though we were all able to laugh about it. We never got to see the hydro races at all.

CHAPTER 8

New Life

When I was not in a marriage, and not worried about Mari, I put my heart and soul into my career. My work became my life. Shortly after moving in with my father, I found a very good job with a private cable and telephone company. I went to California to meet my boss and go through training. Then, with two other guys, we took over a new office in Tukwila, a few miles south of Seattle. It was a very rewarding job, which included sales, marketing and operations. The only downside was the commute: from Marysville to Tukwila, which took about two hours each way in traffic. Ridiculous! Soon I went into the office later to avoid some of the traffic and stayed much later than my coworkers. Then I decided to sleep in a large walk-in closet in the office. I thought that was a pretty clever idea. My boss soon told me I could not do that due to company liability. I knew she was right.

It seemed Mari and Max were doing well. They had been together for years now. Mari was now 24, and Max was 25. They had times when they got into some big arguments and broke up; but they worked through it – sometimes with me getting a phone call from Mari, crying. Max seemed to be angry, most of the time – like his father had been with his mother. Mari was non-confrontational. She would avoid talking about things just to avoid an argument, unlike her mother, me.

NEW LIFE

They had wanted to have children; but Mari was told by her doctor that she may never be able to have children. She had a lot of female problems. There was still no real talk of marriage – not that it would have made any difference. But they were not being careful, with the hope of getting pregnant someday soon. I had no input in the matter. Of course I wanted to be a grandmother, but I really wasn't sure their relationship could last with all their ups and downs and felt it would be wise for them to wait.

Little did I know that Mari and Max were not getting along as well as I had hoped. Mari decided to end the relationship and move to Phoenix to live with her dad until she could find a new job and apartment. Her father and stepmother were ok with that idea. The cost of living was much lower in Phoenix than Seattle. She also was a licensed Pharmacy A Tech, which was much more advanced than Pharmacy Techs in Arizona. She was sure she would do well there. She drove her car down, with a girlfriend along to help her drive. Mari needed a car there. She was very proud of that car. It was the second one that her grandfather had helped her buy. He really did spoil her.

It seemed like Mari was there not quite a month when she called me at work to announce that she was pregnant. I was going to be a grandmother! I was beyond ecstatic! Mari had been sick almost immediately when she arrived at her dad's.

She thought she had the flu. Her stepmom, however, knew better and had her take a home pregnancy test. Sure enough, she was pregnant! She also called Max to let him know. We both wanted her to come back home. This was a little déjà vu for me – reminding me of my pregnancy with her – and I could understand why she would hope to have things work out with Max. I think everyone felt it was best for Mari to come back to Seattle, including her dad and stepmom.

I took some time off work and flew to Phoenix to help Mari drive her car home. It was good to have some alone time, the two of us. She was tired most of the drive. At least she didn't have morning sickness the whole way. I did the driving which was a little stressful; but I was fine. It would have been a perfect opportunity for Mari and me to talk about her pregnancy, her life with or without Max, and how she felt about her life at the time; but I could see she just wanted to sleep. Mari always slept in the car on long trips. I'm sure her pregnancy made her even more tired and was probably relieved that her mom had come to help her.

I had a beautiful, two-story apartment in Edmonds and had Mari move in the apartment with me. I had the upstairs bedroom and bath; Mari had the main floor bedroom and bath. The relationship between Mari and Max was still a little uneasy. But we made plans to get ready for the new baby coming; and we were all excited.

NEW LIFE

She had two great baby showers: I had one and a girlfriend had the other. Mari was back to work as a Pharmacy A Tech and doing well even with her growing belly. Mari tried to get Max to go to childbirth classes, and he did – for just a short time. I didn't know at the time that Max cheated on her quite a bit while Mari was pregnant. She even knew one of the women Max dated, an old girlfriend of Mari's.

When Mari went into labor, Max and I took her to the hospital. Max's mom was there as well. It was such an incredible, very emotional event to see my daughter give birth to her first-born son. She named him Riley. He was gorgeous. It was more emotional for me to see the birth of my grandson than it had been for me to give birth to Mari twenty-five years earlier. Maybe because I was not the one going into labor and delivering. It was just such a wonderful moment for all of us. Max was also a very proud father.

Mari was still very cautious about moving in with Max again, even though they were parents now, so she and baby Riley lived alone with me for a while. I was so in love with this beautiful baby. I was such a proud grandma. And Riley was such a good baby. He seemed to hardly ever cry. And he had his days and nights completely backwards. Mari was so afraid that something would happen to him at night if she fell asleep, so she would put him in his little car seat, on her bed next to her.

Riley would be just wide awake at night – never making a sound. And, of course, he would sleep during the day, so Mari would go in and check on him constantly. She learned, for a while anyway, to sleep when Riley did – until she could get his days and nights straightened out. Riley was only a few weeks old for his first Christmas. He was so tiny. I bought him a miniature Radio Flyer red wagon for Christmas and we put him in the wagon. It was the perfect size for a tiny baby. We took lots of pictures that Christmas. We were so excited to have this beautiful new baby. Max was quite proud too. We could all see he was so thrilled to be a father.

I talked my boss into letting me operate the office from my apartment. The company had already laid off my two co-workers, so I was the only western Washington employee. I was given a promotion to my biggest title and position ever, Regional Market Operations Manager, over the northern California, Oregon and Washington region. I loved working at home. I thought I would be lazy at home, drag myself to my computer slowly - in my pajamas with a coffee cup in hand - and drag through the day. I surprised myself. I was up early, dressed and working every day by 8 am. And I had a hard time pulling myself away from my desk, sometimes even as late as 10 pm. But I did well. And I was proud of my work accomplishments. I loved the heck out of that job. I had to travel once and a while, but not often.

NEW LIFE

I had moved Mari and Riley's room into the large dining room, just like my sister and her first boyfriend had when I moved in with them in Phoenix for a short time. We still had room for the dining room table and chairs. I made the room that was Mari and Riley's into my office. It was beautiful and worked well for all I needed to do from home. I loved our lives.

Mari and Riley moved into Max's apartment once Mari felt good about their relationship again. She was excited about having a family.

Call it the luck of the Irish, Murphy's law, whatever, but it seemed just as I was doing great, and the company appeared to be doing well, the company decided to consolidate the region one more time. They wanted me to move to Oregon. I said no. I had my family in Washington and was now a grandmother. There was no way I would miss a moment being with my daughter and grandson. I gave my notice and looked for a new job, again. I was disappointed to give up that wonderful job; but I knew I would find another good one. I trusted in God and had confidence in my experience and skills.

CHAPTER 9

A Good Marriage

Surprisingly it didn't take any time at all to find a new job. I had a good resume with all my telecommunications experience. The job was in downtown Seattle, an easy bus ride from my neighborhood in Edmonds. It was a relaxing way to get to work. The job was with a company that produced software to be used by analog cell phone companies. The software detected and stopped cloning of people's cell phone identification, stopping cell phone fraud. I was hired as a help desk administrator. Most of the people who worked there were brilliant. Many had doctorates. To say I was under-educated would be an understatement. Everyone was very friendly; and I enjoyed my job.

I met a blind man there, Lonnie, one day when I went outside to have a cigarette on the loading dock in the back of the building. He was quite interesting to talk with. One of his dear, long-time friends, Fred, worked with us; and he walked out with Lonnie to have a smoke break. They both smoked pipes. I was impressed with how Lonnie functioned and maneuvered so well as a blind man. Lonnie also was a true hippie, a long-haired, long-bearded, scruffy-clothes hippie. I had never met anyone like him. He was truly brilliant.

When we first met, Lonnie told me the story of how he became blind. He had Retinitis Pigmentosa.

It's a genetic eye disease that gradually deteriorates the retina. There is currently no cure or treatment for it. He learned that he had it when he was in the Navy and fell on the ship, nearly killing himself, because he couldn't see peripherally. When he went home on leave, he described to his mother what had happened. She said she was sorry to tell him that she had the disease and was going blind herself. She hoped that it would never affect him or his brother; but it obviously had.

Lonnie and I became good friends. He was funny, smart and easy to talk with. I was really attracted to his mind, not his looks. This was new for me. He asked me to go to lunch, then dinner. I learned quickly how to help him walk around downtown Seattle, using his cane. He lived in an apartment right across the street from our office. Lonnie didn't attempt to cook, so we ate out most of the time - a new experience for me. We had fun.

I still had my beautiful apartment in Edmonds. I spent many times during the week, at Lonnie's apartment. Within a year or so, though, the company we both worked for was closing. It was a time when the cell phone industry was changing from analog to digital phones; and the software the company provided to cell phone companies was becoming obsolete. The company had not prepared for that change, even though Lonnie had tried to prepare them. He was a senior software engineer; but upper management didn't heed his warning.

It turned out, I found out much into my dating Lonnie, that he had written all the software that ran the company! He had brought it with him when he started with the company. I knew he was brilliant; but I had no idea how brilliant until I heard that story. And I only found this out from his friend Fred. Lonnie was much too humble to tell me.

I was laid off before Lonnie, so I went to work for another telecommunications company as an account manager, selling long-distance service. The office was also downtown; but I went there only for meetings. Most of the time I traveled around the Seattle metro area, selling. I learned quickly that I loved marketing; but I certainly didn't like sales, especially cold calling.

When Lonnie left the company, one of the last to leave, we moved him out of his downtown Seattle apartment and into mine in Edmonds. He asked me to quit the job I disliked, if I wanted to. Lonnie had a comfortable income for the two of us to live on. He had already retired from his previous job, prior to working for the one where we met, so he had his retirement to live on. This was the first time in my adult life I didn't have to work. It was such a luxury. I had worked two jobs at times to make ends meet while raising Mari.

Lonnie and I were very happy and comfortable with each other. I was falling in love with him. For the first time I was in love with someone for who they were inside. I was so beyond picking a mate based on their looks.

I knew this relationship was different. Lonnie and I loved having Mari, Max and Riley over. Riley was growing like crazy. He was such a beautiful, happy baby. I can remember him eating solid foods for the first time. Mari and I filmed it with their video camera. It was such a treat. And he was so excited to eat – his hands and feet were going everywhere! When Riley was a little over a year old, Mari and Max announced they were going to have another baby, a girl. We were so excited for them. How perfect, a boy and a girl. And the age difference between the two children, nearly two years, could be good for the kids and their parents' sanity. Max and Mari were very excited too. And they seemed to be getting along so well. Both had good jobs and a nice apartment in Seattle. We were thrilled for them.

Even though I liked to cook, Lonnie and I loved going out to nice restaurants for dinner. One night, while we were having a fabulous dinner out, Lonnie said, "So how long do we have to live together before we get married?" I was surprised. I didn't know he was thinking about marriage. I answered him with a smart aleck comment, "Is that your way of asking me to marry you?" He said, "Yes. And I'm afraid that's about as romantic as I get." I just laughed. It was very true, I learned. Lonnie was not a romantic man at all; but he was sure a loving, giving, patient man. We planned to marry.

I had Mari's baby shower at our apartment. We had so much fun. Mari's friends and co-workers all came. Mari received so many wonderful gifts. Mari was huge; she had gained more weight than she had with her first pregnancy with Riley. Mari's Ob-Gyn watched Mari carefully and was sure the pregnancy would go just fine.

Mari and Max had their baby girl, Shea, just twenty-two months after Riley was born. The delivery didn't go as smoothly as everyone planned. The doctor decided to do an emergency C section, as Shea was in distress during the delivery. But Shea was just fine. She was a beautiful, healthy baby. Mari, on the other hand, had some complications after the delivery and had to go back to the hospital for a few days. She was so upset that she couldn't be at home with her babies.

Shea was born nine months before Lonnie and I got married. Our little grandchildren looked so cute all dressed up in their little suit and dress at the wedding. Mari and Max had a beautiful family. I was so proud and happy for them.

Our wedding was simple but beautiful. I had help decorating the hall we rented. We had many close friends and family. I was so proud of my soon-to-be husband coming down the aisle. We had bought him a sharp looking, new suit for the wedding. He even agreed to have his silver-grey beard and mustache trimmed, and his long hair pulled back neatly in a ponytail. He looked so handsome.

One of his best friends walked him down the aisle; and my father walked me down the aisle to meet him in front of the minister. It was the third marriage for each of us. I finally knew this was the right marriage. I had no doubt about this man.

This was such a totally different marriage from my first two. I knew this time I was marrying a man I loved and who loved me. I finally trusted my instinct and my heart!

We went to Hawaii for two weeks for our honeymoon. I had never had a real honeymoon in my two previous marriages. We went with a couple that Lonnie had known for years, another blind man and his wife. They had a time-share condo in Kona. We stayed there for a week, then we all went to Oahu and stayed in a large hotel on Waikiki Beach. We preferred the big island and Kona, with its quiet and relaxing views from the condo. We could hear the waves day and night from our condo even though it was five blocks from the beach. In Waikiki Beach, our large high-rise hotel was right on the beach; yet the noise of the traffic on the strip was so loud, we could never hear the ocean. We truly had a wonderful time in Hawaii. Lonnie and I even parasailed together one day.

Lonnie and I lived in the apartment in Edmonds for another year or so after we married. It was a beautiful apartment, in a fantastic neighborhood, close to any store or restaurant we needed. Lonnie still amazed me at how well he had adapted to this place, finding his way around each room. I'm sure he was lost without his computer though. We needed to set one up for him, as software scripting was his life, so he could keep his mind going.

We saw Mari, Max, Riley and Shea as often as we could, either at our apartment or theirs. We hosted Shea's first birthday party for family at our place, even though Mari and Max would have the kids' party at Chuck E Cheese or McDonald's. It was so fun to see the kids grow up. They were so precious. Shea was born with a little bit of an 'attitude' though. If she didn't like something, she would make a sound like, "hum" and stomp her foot. Even when she was a baby, she would make this funny noise, instead of crying sometimes, like she was disgusted. I can remember Mari saying, "What the hell is that?" when Shea did that for the first time. We all cracked up laughing. Shea's attitude wasn't anything her parents couldn't handle though; and we all laughed at it often which, of course, made Shea more upset.

Riley was so happy, even-tempered and cuddly. He was a super big brother to Shea as well. We had his third birthday at our house as well, after going to the customary kids' party at McDonalds. We took a gazillion pictures of the kids. We just couldn't get enough of them. Lonnie had some grandkids from his previous two marriages; but they lived out of state and he hadn't seen them in years.

We went to Mari and Max's one Christmas to spend it with the kids. It was so fun. There is nothing like seeing little kids get excited on Christmas morning! And they were always so good, excited and grateful for everything they got.

They were everything to us, and life seemed to be stable for everyone. It was a happy time. Max and Mari were doing well in their relationship and got engaged again! Lonnie and I were so happy for them. They seemed like the perfect little family. Max also really liked Lonnie and thought of him like a father.

Lonnie and I went to Anacortes one day to see a long-time friend of his. He and his wife and daughter lived on a beach there. They owned the property, which consisted of a main house and a smaller beach house on a little hill above the main house. They had been renting the small house out to someone who planned to leave soon, so Lonnie's friends asked us if we'd like to rent it. It sounded wonderful. I had always wanted to live on the beach. I just loved being close to the water: it was my perfect place. The little house wasn't quite on the beach, but we could see it from the house perfectly; and we had complete freedom to go down to the beach past the main house anytime. We knew it would be easy to give the landlord our notice to leave the apartment and decided to rent this beautiful, little beach house.

CHAPTER 10

Ahh...The Beach

We moved into the little beach house and were so excited to find that our family – Mari and Max and the kids, and my sister and her husband – loved to come and visit us, often spending the weekends. It was only a two-bedroom, one bath, little 800 square-foot home; but we made room for family when they came up for little "weekend vacations". It was such a beautiful area. And we had an incredible view of the water from our living room/dining room entire wall of windows. We walked down to the beach any time we wanted. We had a very nice brick patio and large, grassy back yard. The kids just loved playing in the yard and on the beach. Riley was four and Shea two. They were so much fun.

We set up one of the two bedrooms as an office for Lonnie. It had taken a while to get what Lonnie wanted; but he finally had the computer equipment, talking software, and room to do all the software engineering he wanted. He was in heaven. He found some incredible talk shows and music stations from around the world that he would listen to at night. I really enjoyed the music stations, especially those with new acid jazz.

For Shea's second birthday, I acquired a child's battery-operated little car, a Corvette, from my sister. It had been their daughter's car; and she had outgrown it many years earlier.

AHH... THE BEACH

I spray painted it gold, got a personalized license plate with Shea's name on it, and put a new battery in it. She was so excited when she opened this great big present with a big bow on it. The kids, especially Shea, had a wonderful time playing with it, driving it all over the place. I also made a new doll house out of one I found at a garage sale and put new furniture, carpet and wallpaper in it for Shea. She was only two at the time, way too young to appreciate the doll house. She destroyed it in no time.

We had BBQ parties there for the kids, with Mari and Max inviting many of their friends who had kids Riley and Shea's age. It seemed like the sun was always shining there. Odd, for the Northwest. It was just such a beautiful place.

We had my 50th birthday party at the beach house. We invited family and friends over, which now included a lot of the neighbors on that beach street. It was fun to have people over and celebrate our time together.

We also had Mari's 30th birthday party there. We had invited family and friends, as always. But I had an even greater surprise planned for Mari. We had Mari's grandmother, her dad's mother, flown up to surprise her. And I also invited Mari's dad, Allen, to come. I called him to invite him, rather nervous to even speak to him since it had been years since we spoke; but to everyone's surprise, he came. Mari was so surprised to have her grandmother and father there. It was a wonderful surprise for her.

It was probably the biggest celebration of Mari, ever. This was the first time Allen got to meet his two grandchildren, Riley and Shea. He was quite thrilled with them, and even acted like a proud grandpa. Mom (my ex mother-in-law) and Allen both stayed for a few days and left. Allen, of course, made his great promises to stay in touch with Mari, as he always had in the past. I'm sure Mari believed he would keep his promise this time.

Lonnie and I stayed in that little beach house for over a year. We were told by a neighbor that she had a friend who owned a large house on nearby Whidbey Island that could be for rent. We got in touch with owner. He planned to fly out from back east to see what needed to be done to rent it again. We saw it and loved it, even though it required a huge clean-up and repair process. The owner had come out earlier in the year to start the fix-up process but left right in the middle of it to go back to the east coast. We decided to move into the bigger house so that more family could stay with us, in their own bedrooms. I spent days working with the owner to get it ready for us to move in. The house was huge compared to the little beach house we had in Anacortes. It had five bedrooms, three downstairs, two upstairs, three baths, a huge family room with a fireplace downstairs and a gorgeous living room with cathedral ceilings, a slate stone fireplace and floor-to-ceiling windows that had a 180-degree view of Puget Sound and Mount Baker on the main floor!

AHH... THE BEACH

The kitchen and dining room had windows on three sides of the room – also with an incredible view of the Sound. The upstairs, main living area of the house, had a huge deck outside that ran the full width of the house. What an incredible house. We sat out on that deck many days and nights. The house was on a bluff overlooking a bay on Whidbey, so we felt like we were sitting in a special seating area with the Sound, Mount Baker and all the amazing natural views laid out in front of us, just for our viewing!

Even though Lonnie was blind and couldn't see all the beauty surrounding us there, he enjoyed sitting outside on the upper-level deck, listening to the sounds of nature, or listening to one of his favorite talk radio shows, and smoking his pipe and drinking a beer. I would sit outside with him sometimes at night and look at all the stars. I felt like we were surrounded by the stars, everywhere. It was gorgeous. One night, I looked up at the clouds and they started moving, in a funny way. I'd never seen anything like this. I tried to describe to Lonnie how they moved. The clouds looked like they were moving in waves and squiggles, as if they were dancing for us. Lonnie told me I was watching the Northern Lights! They continued for what seemed like hours, although I'm sure it really wasn't that long. I was absolutely mesmerized! It was a spiritual experience for me. I felt like God was putting on this incredible light show just for me. I'll never forget that first experience, even though I saw the Northern Lights at least three more times while we lived there on Whidbey.

CHAPTER 11

Meanwhile She Keeps Dancing

Mari's had a plaque on a wall in her home forever that reads, "She gets up. She falls down. Meanwhile she keeps dancing." It's her mantra.

Mari and Max and the kids stayed with us often at the house on Whidbey. The kids loved it because it had great outside areas in which to play. They also had their own bedrooms, with their own toys and play areas. It was like they had their own house downstairs.

But Mari and Max were up and down in their relationship, more down times than I actually knew about at the time. Mari was busy working, taking care of their home and being a mother, so she didn't have a lot of time to tell me how she and Max were doing. So, most of the time, I thought "no news is good news."

Just when they planned to break up, they discovered they were expecting another baby. It had happened that way when Mari found out she was pregnant with Riley and Shea both; and now they discovered they were pregnant with their third child, another boy. I don't think they were as happy about this pregnancy this time, simply because they were so ready to end their relationship. I could tell Mari was stressed and unhappy. Max seemed angry. They were hardly speaking to each other.

They had their beautiful little boy, Bentley, in September. It seemed Max took to this baby more than he had with the first two.

I'm sure he loved them just as much as Bentley; he just didn't want to put him down. They came up to the house with all three kids to celebrate Thanksgiving and Christmas that year, but broke up, for good, just shortly after that. They had been living in a house in North Seattle for about a year when Bentley was born. They just couldn't make it work, after thirteen years of being together. Bentley would spend his life without his parents living together.

They decided not to take any parenting agreements to court; they mutually agreed to share custody of the kids. Mari wanted to make sure that the children would always have a good relationship with their father so that they would never have to experience what she had gone through without a relationship with her father. The kids seemed to do ok with this arrangement. I don't think Mari did though. She was thirty-one now and felt like her beautiful family life was gone.

I believe this was the time when Mari began to drink. I don't think I saw Mari drink very much in the past, ever, other than when she got drunk on the Seafair cruise, fell and had a concussion. She and I would talk on the phone and she would tell me how upset she was about not having her kids full time. I could tell she didn't sound like herself; I knew she was calling me drunk. I would listen to her and tell her that she made the right choice in sharing custody of the kids with Max, so the kids could have their father in their lives; but I couldn't convince her that having the kids only part-time did not mean her life was over.

I knew Mari was unhappy with the Max breakup; but she was devastated about the idea that she wouldn't have the kids to herself full time. She had tried so hard to make the relationship work with Max. She wanted to have the happy family life; and it just wasn't going to happen.

Mari attempted suicide one more time, the fourth. It was alcohol-fueled. She called me crying, saying she had taken some pills again. We were still living on Whidbey Island and Mari was in Seattle, two hours away. I couldn't run to her right away because of the distance, so I called 911 and an ambulance took her to the hospital. She was in an in-patient facility for a week, then in out-patient therapy for two weeks.

Visiting her was awkward. It felt like she didn't want to see me. I'm sure she felt a lot of pain, maybe even anger at me for not helping her more. I lived so far away from her at that time. And, like always, I didn't know what to say or do to comfort or help her. I just wanted her to be ok. I felt helpless again. My daughter felt like her life, her dreams of having a loving, happy family life, was over. I felt like she wanted to die and there was nothing I could do to help her. She told me later that she felt like I had chosen to spend time with my husband and he took priority over her in my life. That hurt. Lonnie was very important to me. He was independent; but I still needed to be there for him. I had experienced Mari's three suicide attempts before; and I still could not figure out what I could say or do to help her. I had learned over the years there was nothing I could do for her by myself.

Nothing I could say to her would fix her feelings about her life. I felt in-patient therapy was the best place for her to be. She had felt abandoned so many times by Max and now she felt like she was losing her children. She did not though.

Mari continued with therapy as often as she could. Sometimes it was difficult for her to take time off from work; but she tried to see a therapist at least once a month. Her focus was on being a healthy mother for her kids. She wanted to have them full time; but she also didn't want to keep the kids from their dad. She wanted a good life for them.

When Mari appeared to be doing much better emotionally, she met a young man, Sam, who was in the Navy and stationed at the base in Everett. Lonnie and I met him a few times. He seemed nice; but we didn't see them often. Mari and Sam were happy, at first anyway. They became engaged after being together for a year. They moved into Sam's apartment together, one that had a separate bedroom for the kids when they came for their week with Mari. It didn't take long, however, for Mari to realize that Sam had more of a drinking problem than she did. He was a nice guy, with a drinking problem. She stopped drinking just so that the two of them would not be raging drunk together. She was attracting unhealthy relationships still. I think she saw that, maybe a little too late. Mari kept working in her pharmacy job, at a hospital, while she was in the relationship with Sam. She was laid off, however, just as the relationship was ending. Mari had given up her apartment to move in with Sam, so she had no place to go.

CHAPTER 12

Our Time by the Lake

Lonnie and I rented houses in Anacortes, then Whidbey Island, trying to decide where we wanted to buy a home. We considered buying the house we were renting on Whidbey, but we also knew after living there for a couple years that the house would require a lot of money to fix up. We started looking around. Everything we looked at that we could afford needed a lot of work or had a terrible layout.

Some friends of ours who lived on Camano Island recommended we look in their neighborhood. We found a home near a lake with a large lot and just the right amount of space for the two of us and family that would like to come to visit. The front yard was large and so beautifully landscaped that it looked like a park. The front deck was appealing as well. Lonnie loved the layout of the house. He never ceased to amaze me at how he could get used to the layout of a house so quickly! I don't think I could have ever functioned well as a blind person. In fact, I'm sure of it. I would have been so frustrated and impatient. He was such a laid back, patient man.

We bought the house. It struck me, after we moved in, that the beautiful park-like front yard was going to be a huge maintenance project for me.

OUR TIME BY THE LAKE

We bought a gas-powered push mower for me to use, even though Lonnie kept telling me, "I really think you're going to need a riding mower, or you'll be out there for hours!" I countered that suggestion, saying, "If we have to pay that much for a riding lawn mower, we should be able to drive it down the street like a car because they cost nearly as much!" After attempting to use the push mower for the first time, which took me two days to mow just the front yard, I conceded. We returned the mower and bought a riding mower. I loved riding it every time I had to mow the grass. It was relaxing and fun.

When Mari and Sam broke up, she moved out of Sam's apartment and into our house on Camano Island. It was quite a distance to any pharmacy job Mari could get; but she looked. In the interim, though, she took a little break from working. But this also meant she had to rearrange her time with the kids, so they could go to their daycare in the Seattle area and the two older kids could go to school. Max still lived in Seattle and took the kids during the week and Mari had them, at our house, on the weekends. This was so tough on Mari, not seeing the kids during the week. With no job or kids to keep her afloat, she was sinking again and started drinking more.

We decided to add a deck and screened-in porch on the back of the house so that Lonnie would have a safe and relaxing place to go every night to listen to his talk radio shows, smoke his pipe and drink his beer.

Lonnie was a "maintenance" alcoholic. He could drink a lot; but he only drank at home. He made a promise to me when we got married that he would drink only at home, other than a cocktail at restaurants when we went out for dinner. He knew when to stop or he could lose his equilibrium and, without vision, could fall and hurt himself. He scared me one time going up the stairs to our apartment in Edmonds, and nearly fell down the stairs. He was six feet tall and around two hundred pounds, so I knew I could not stop him from falling or pick him up if he fell. That's when I told him I could not handle his drinking outside of our home. He was careful not to drink too much and was usually in bed before midnight. Lonnie was a happy, mellow alcoholic. This is when Mari built a new relationship with Lonnie, her step-father, while she was living with us. Mari would sit outside and drink beer and smoke cigarettes with Lonnie. The two most important people in my life were both alcoholics.

I really didn't have a lot of experience in my lifetime with alcoholism. Neither of my parents drank much, other than a glass of wine when they had company once and a while. No one else in my family really drank. Even I didn't drink much. I started to drink when I moved to Phoenix after high school, to go to college, and learned a few times that getting drunk was not fun. I always liked to feel I was in control of my thoughts and my body. For Mari and Lonnie, it was different; and I learned to tolerate this. We had a good life there on Camano.

Mari stayed with us for two years; and the kids were there every weekend. We had fun with them. They loved playing in the large yard. It seemed to be a retreat for them.

My sister and brother-in-law came up to visit us from Everett as often as they could as well. They loved our quiet, relaxing rural neighborhood. We had so much fun with them, and they enjoyed seeing our grandkids. They didn't have any grandkids of their own yet. In fact, it wasn't until Riley was six years old that their son married; Riley was in their wedding. The grandkids came many years later for them.

Mari was not happy living with us. I could tell. She didn't have her kids full-time; she didn't have her own apartment. Lonnie's office was her bedroom. She was stressed. I realized that it's very difficult for an adult child to move back home, especially with kids of her own, and feel like she has any control. She found a job in Seattle, working for a big insurance company in a department that used her many years of pharmacy experience. She commuted from a park and ride near the freeway in Stanwood, all the way to downtown Seattle and back each day. This was a long commute for her, over an hour each way; but the bus ride saved her a lot of money and wear and tear on her car. She did this until she had enough money to move back to the Seattle area and have the kids during the week. I knew she was relieved to find an apartment for her and the kids and get back to every-other-week custody sharing with Max. She could finally have a place of her own and the kids with her more, again.

When Mari moved to her own apartment in Seattle, I decided to take an Interior Redesign course in Victoria, B.C. Interior Redesign was different from full Interior Design in that the designer worked with what the clients already had in their home, moving and rearranging furniture, accessories and art in many rooms to make the clients' home look new. It was also a trending service for real estate staging for home sales. There was a method and process to this service. It was something I had done many times in my own homes, and for my family, for many years. I always loved Interior Design and had taken some classes in the past but had not completed the course. I had even worked a second, part-time job as a design consultant at a furniture store when Mari was in high school. It was a passion for me.

Becoming certified in this field made me feel confident in starting my own business as a designer. I had many clients and I loved it. I even had Mari help me with some redesign clients. We worked well together. She was a natural at it as well.

When Mari lived on her own with the kids, she had problems with Bentley crying uncontrollably sometimes. He had done this often at our house as well, even as a baby. He would scream; and no one could calm him down. He wasn't hungry, tired or in pain. And holding him would not help. It was very stressful for Mari and tested my patience when he was with us. We didn't know what to do for him.

The only thing that could calm him down was his 'Johnny Jump-up', a spring-loaded seat that could be attached to the top of a door frame. He would bounce up and down in that thing for hours, and usually fall asleep.

Mari didn't drink at all when she was pregnant with any of the three kids, but she had been on anti-depressants when she found out she was pregnant with Bentley. Her Ob-Gyn had recommended that she stay on the anti-depressants during her pregnancy because stopping them could be worse for the baby. We think the anti-depressants may have affected Bentley, causing his outbursts. It was hard for any of us to deal with his screaming, most of all Mari. Her pediatrician had no suggestions.

It wasn't until Bentley started kindergarten that a teacher suggested, after only a week or so in school, that Bentley had ADD or ADHD and was not ready for school. Mari took him out of school and back into full-time daycare. He had to wait one year to start school, although Mari was very uncomfortable about this. As soon as he started school the next year, his teacher asked why he was in kindergarten. Mari explained what had happened with Bentley the previous year. This teacher said, "He needs to be in first grade, with the other children his age. He's very smart." And he was. He moved up to first grade.

He did have disruptive times in school though, typical of ADHD. Mari had him tested that year and he was within the spectrum of ADHD.

She put him on medication for that for a while. But Bentley said he didn't like how he felt on those drugs. Mari did not want to drug her child, so she took him off them within a year. Bentley did ok without the drugs. Mari was so loving and patient with him - with all three kids, even though she was very stressed.

I did some research and believed he had Sensory Processing Disorder (SPD). I had a close friend whose son had SPD. His behavior sounded just like Bentley's. I called a medical center in Everett that specialized in SPD and talked with a specialist about his behavior. They used therapy with the children, not drugs. I gave this information to Mari, hoping she could have him tested and possibly treated there. Mari didn't pursue that SPD center, and I'm not sure why.

Bentley was six now. I spent some time teaching him how to meditate, showing him how to visualize the calming scene he could create in his mind. We called it the "calming exercise" and hoped he could use this process to calm himself whenever he could feel an outburst or uncontrollable energy coming up in school. I talked to the principal at the kids' school about my hope to assist some of the teachers who were encountering issues with kids like Bentley in their classes. My plan was to start working with the teachers the following year. However, I was unable to do this because of a serious issue that came up with Lonnie.

Now that Mari had the kids with her more, had a good job and lived in her own apartment again, she seemed to be doing well. The kids were doing well in school, all three of them.

She came to visit us, usually for one of the kids' birthdays, or for some other family occasion; but she was very busy. With three kids, of course she would be. And sometimes she was very stressed and would call me. She was stressed about her lack of money, the kids and her lack of a love life. She was trying to handle her full life. I would talk with her about how she had a good life, even though it was stressful being a single mother. She would tell me that I had no idea what she was going through. I said, "Of course I do. I raised you completely by myself." But she said, "There's no comparison between raising one child and raising three!" I agreed, but then proceeded to completely tick her off by saying, "but no one told you to have three children when you knew your relationship was not good." That wasn't fair; but it was true. It reminded me of what my mother said to me about "being so stupid when it came to men." I felt horrible for saying it. I listened to her pain; but I also felt like she wanted more from me. I just didn't know what it was. I couldn't fix her life for her. I think she wanted me to be there with her (in person) when she was upset. Maybe she just "needed her Mommy" as she would say sometimes. It just wasn't possible to get there most of the time she called me. I also think that was a time when she was very much teetering between drinking and not drinking.

Mari really was a good mother. She had more patience with them than I had sometimes.

I knew from the time I was a child that I lacked patience. Mari didn't. She talked to them from the time they were babies like they were little adults. She had cute little nick-names for each of them: Riley was Buddy; Shea was Missy; and Bentley was Muffin. They were good kids. She didn't tolerate any talking back or bad behavior, or they were in a time-out. And she wasn't overprotective with her kids, which she could have been considering what she had experienced as a child.

She always made sure she had excellent daycare providers for the kids. They were like family to the kids. The first two kids went to an older, very loving, but strict, woman everyone called Aunt Ellen. She was awesome and had come recommended by one of Mari's girlfriends who had gone to her daycare when she was a child. The kids, along with Bentley just after he was born, went to a new daycare when Aunt Ellen retired. That was also wonderful for the kids. For years the kids at that daycare all went to the same school, took the school bus and spent the afternoons together while waiting for their parents to pick them up. Many older kids, like Riley and Shea, helped take care of the little ones, like Bentley, when they could, even though the daycare had a good, large staff.

Mari concentrated on losing weight after she had Bentley. She gained more weight each time she had a child but lost most of it each time. Over the years it got harder and harder for her to lose weight.

But she did it. I think working, and having coworkers dieting as well helped her get back to her tiny, petite self. She looked good; and she certainly didn't look like she was in her mid-thirties.

Mari had some good girlfriends she could rely on in this period in her life. A couple of them wanted Mari to go on a vacation with them to New Orleans for a few days, kind of pre-Mardi Gras time. This was her first vacation from the kids. She and Max had gone camping a lot when Riley and Shea were little; but this was her time alone with her girlfriends. Mari got Max to keep the kids while she was gone. She was having a wonderful time. I talked with her a few times on the phone. The last time I called her, however, was to tell her that she needed to come home right away, if she could. Her grandfather was dying.

CHAPTER 13

Her Grandpa

A few years after my mom passed away, Beth and Ross, my sister and brother-in-law, moved my dad into their home in Everett. It was a small, older home; but they made room for Dad because they felt he needed to live with someone, no longer on his own. He was in his eighties. Dad was doing amazingly well after my mom's death though. I think he liked living with them. My sister had such patience, more than I could have ever conjured up. Dad was a little "fuss budget" as they used to say, always fussing over someone or something, something I couldn't have handled. And Ross had a problem with that at times as well. Dad had a lot of arthritis; but he got around quite well, and still drove, which we objected to for years. His driving was quite scary! When he had two accidents in the same parking lot at one time, we insisted he quit driving. And he did. We could tell this limited him tremendously, taking away his independence.

Beth and Ross decided to research senior apartments for Dad. They found a new senior apartment complex in downtown Everett. We all helped Dad move in. It wasn't great; but it gave him his independence and his own place. It wasn't an assisted living facility, but a multi-level complex where he could meet people his age. It reminded me of a hotel room, only with his own furniture.

Dad had a female friend, June, that he had known for years (my mother knew her as well when she was alive) who took him places. Dad loved this. He had quite a crush on June really. It was cute to see. He would always say it was just platonic. In fact, Dad had been quite a flirt all my life; but it was always totally respectful and innocent. So it was quite a shock when we he told us that he and June got married! He didn't tell us until after he got married. Beth and I were pretty upset about that – not that he got married – but that he waited to tell us afterward. They moved into a two-bedroom apartment together, in the same senior building in which he lived.

Just when Mari was feeling good about her life, and on a long-needed vacation, she got the news that her grandpa was dying. His illness, a stomach or bowel blockage that couldn't be removed because of my dad's age and heart risks, had come up very suddenly. Beth and I had no idea this had been going on at all. Dad and June had been married for just a few months; and we hadn't seen much of him.

I remember going to see him in the hospital at first, thinking that this was something that could be surgically removed, or worked out with drugs, and that it wasn't too serious. In fact, I didn't tell Mari about her grandpa being ill at first because I thought he would be just fine. He was only in the hospital for tests then. Next thing we knew, he was under Hospice care at home with drug therapy just to make him comfortable.

My sister, my niece Allison, and myself were all taking turns being by my dad's side as he was dying. His wife, June, was there but allowed us to stay by his side most of the time. There were times when he was in and out of consciousness; and there were a couple times that we believe he was trying to describe to us what he was seeing. I'm sure he was between this earth and going to 'the other side'. He described seeing our mother, saying how beautiful she was. It was a beautiful experience to be by his side and hear these descriptions, yet a sad time for us, knowing that Dad didn't have very long to live. When he became somewhat combative and difficult for the family to keep him in bed and comfortable with his medication, Hospice recommended he be taken back to the hospital. We learned from Hospice that end-of-life mediations can be difficult to adjust to make the patient comfortable at home. That's when I decided I needed to call Mari and have her come home.

This was shocking and devastating news for Mari. She worshipped her grandpa. She had only been gone a few days; but she flew home as quickly as she could get a flight. We girls - Beth, Allison, and me – were all by Dad's side at the hospital, constantly watching his every breath, thinking it would be his last. But Dad hung in until Mari appeared by his side, sometime early the next morning. Mari got to tell him how much she loved him and said goodbye.

HER GRANDPA

My dad, as I said earlier, was an incredible man. He was the most giving, loving, caring man I had ever known. He was especially kind and loving to Mari. I believe he tried to play the father role for her since she grew up without her father. He had played with Mari so much when she was little. I have pictures he took of Mari standing in their living room, at age two, in her little two-piece bathing suit, holding on to a rope; something my dad had fixed for her to pretend she was water skiing. He built her a playhouse out of cardboard boxes that she could play in on their enclosed back porch, also when she was little. He helped her buy her first two cars, the first when she was just starting out in college at age sixteen.

He was extremely gentle and giving, especially to the women in his life. He was surrounded by women in his family. He was a true gentleman. It wasn't until he passed away, and I was writing his eulogy, that I realized how little I appreciated what a good man he had been. Mari had told me many times that I didn't "appreciate Grandpa". As I wrote, I realized she was right. We had a grand funeral service at his Catholic church and cemetery - with full Knights of Columbus ceremonial honors, a church full of his friends and full military honors at the cemetery. He deserved all of this. He was an amazing man. And Mari was lost without her grandpa. She had adored her grandparents and now she no longer had either. She now only had her grandmother (her dad's mother) in Texas.

CHAPTER 14

Functioning

Mari still functioned as a mother and as a Pharmacy A Tech; but her social life was not great. I knew she just wasn't happy. I could tell by our phone conversations and when we came down to see her and the kids. She had another relationship that didn't last very long, especially when she found out she was pregnant. She had a tubal pregnancy and made it to the hospital in time to not be in critical danger, but the pregnancy was terminated then. Her life just seemed to be one thing after another. I know she was trying to keep her head afloat; but I don't think she knew how. She was depressed, tired and looked like she didn't care anymore. And her drinking became more prevalent.

I tried to get Mari to read self-help and spiritual books for years, to help her pull herself up and out of the downward spirals. She would always say, "I don't read books. I don't have time." She was still going to counseling whenever she could; but she also refused to go to any AA meetings. I'm sure her counselor suggested she go to AA. I certainly did. I had never been to an AA meeting; but I knew some people who went, and they swore by the meetings. She would say, "I just don't want anyone to tell me I can never have another drink in my life!" Pretty crazy; but I couldn't talk her out of that.

Maybe that's about the time I realized that no matter what I suggested to Mari to help her get her life together, she always dismissed it saying, "Don't have time, don't want to do that," or, "Yeah I know, Mom."

Even years before she and Max were together, when Lynn and Mari were my roommates while they were going to college, I would sit with them and we'd talk for hours about spiritual beliefs. I had developed strong spiritual and metaphysical beliefs beginning in my early twenties; and I wanted to share them with the girls. Lynn loved the talks. Mari, on the other hand, would say "Ok, Mom, that's too woo-woo for me!" And she didn't want to hear any more. I always felt that her soul was crying for help. This was not a religious lecture. I wanted them to understand how each person can find their own spiritual way to a good and happy life. Call it a gut feeling, but I felt like this could be her only way to love herself and find happiness. But she never seemed to be ready to hear this.

I really don't know what occurred, but one day I found out Mari was fired from her good job at the insurance company in downtown Seattle. I'm guessing that her attendance was bad as her alcohol use became more problematic. I don't think she ever went to work drunk. She was a very good worker. I just think she would miss work because of the hangovers and depression, etc. She was emotionally and financially struggling again.

Luckily, Mari found a good job with another insurance company. It was much closer to home as well. She seemed to really excel in this job. I think it had been years since she liked a job. I didn't know this until much later. It turned out she really hated pharmacy work, even though she had been in the field for 23 years. She'd found it very redundant, not at all creative. It had given her a good salary. It was an important profession. She just went through the motions all those years. I was surprised. She'd never really said that in all that time.

Mari worked for this insurance company as a pharmacy specialist for quite a few years. She had always been a hard worker, putting everything she had into her job, even if she disliked pharmacy. She was a leader. She developed some good friendships at that company.

The kids were all doing well in school. Bentley was calming down in school, with few disruptions. He had some good friends from the daycare as he grew up. The kids continued to go to the daycare before and after school, as Max and Mari dropped them off and picked them up before and after their jobs. Mari and Max still had shared custody, one week on and one week off. Shea became involved in a girls' drill team and immediately excelled at that. She instantly demonstrated the discipline she needed to be in a military drill team. Riley was super smart, and always calm and loving.

When Riley was in sixth grade, his teacher demonstrated to the class how to work and explain word math problems. Riley was exceptionally good at math. He could come up with the right answers to the math problems; but he couldn't explain, in writing, how he came up with the answers. The teacher was adamant that it was more important that he show how he came up with the answers than to come up with the correct answers in his head. Taking away the natural ability a child may have to figure a math problem out in his head made us furious! And, just like his mom had experienced when she was that age and was told she couldn't continue to take advanced classes – because the teacher had her own agenda on what was right – Riley lost faith in his ability to figure the answers out on his own, and excel, and lost interest in school. I thought this was criminal and it made me sad for Riley. We tried to boost his confidence in how super smart he was in math.

Time seemed to fly by. The kids were growing up so fast. Shea loved school and her drill team. Her drill team was good and very competitive. They went to state competitions each year Shea was in drill. I went to almost every state competition. Leaving Lonnie for just a couple days was ok when I had all his meals planned and ready for him to heat in the microwave. He really was independent. I just worried about leaving him alone. Luckily, we had a wonderful neighbor on one side of us who kept an eye on him while I was gone.

Shea was also an amazing singer. I don't think I realized how good she was until she sang in a talent competition at her first state competition for drill. These competitions were full weekend events, with many track and field events, drill competitions, a dance on that Saturday evening, a talent show and a huge awards ceremony on the last day. Mari and I were so proud of Shea. She was so disciplined in drill and such a talented singer!

The boys enjoyed the track and field events. They both usually won awards for the events they competed in as well. This was such a great, healthy, competitive weekend for so many kids who came from all around the state. I think this is when Bentley realized he really liked sports.

At the first state competition I attended, at their Saturday night dance, I watched all the kids dance with each other. There weren't many boys there. The kids were having a fantastic time dancing. I noticed that there was one young girl in the middle of the dance floor, dancing by herself and with the girls around her. She had Down Syndrome. Everyone around her was having a blast dancing with her. She was so happy. It made me happy enough to cry with joy, to see her so happy. It also made me realize that these were beautiful, loving kids who placed no judgement on anyone who may be a little different from them. It helped me realize that kids are truly accepting, loving people who only learn to judge, or hate, from adults. It's not in their nature to be anything but loving and kind. They only learn to be mean and cruel from what they see in the world as they grow up.

My grandkids impressed me day by day. I don't think they were any smarter or more talented than Mari had been as a child. I think I was just more in the moment with my grandkids. Riley was still quiet, a deep thinker, an old soul. He was exceptional in drawing, right from the time he picked up a pencil. Mari was the same way when she was a child. Mari and all three kids could draw so well. It was exciting to see the kids grow and excel, and to see Mari just beam with pride! I could see that she took a genuine interest in what her kids were doing and how well they were doing their school work and extracurricular activities, and so did I every chance I had.

Even as the kids were growing so fast, they always loved coming up to stay with Lonnie and me on Camano Island. Sometimes we would keep them for a weekend, just so Mari could have a weekend to herself. We knew she needed it. The kids were good; but they could be a handful sometimes. Riley and Shea always got along just fine; but Shea would often get annoyed with Bentley so easily. She could be mean to him. But the kids truly loved each other. When my sister Beth and I were growing up, I was also very mean to her sometimes. I guess that's just the way it is with siblings.

CHAPTER 15

Lonnie

Lonnie loved having the kids up to visit. He was a quiet, gentle man. He was a deep thinker. He would spend hours and hours, nearly all day, scripting software programs on his computer. He needed that to keep him going, to keep his mind active. And he also loved to record music for me. He loved to record the kids voices when they were little, getting them to say some of the cutest things. And the kids loved their grandpa. He was essentially their only grandpa at that time. They were little when their great-grandpa, my dad, passed away. They didn't get to see their dad's parents, as Max's mom had moved back to Chicago, and his dad had never lived in Washington.

I think because Lonnie was so quiet, the kids were a little unsure of him. And maybe it was simply because he was blind; and the kids didn't know how to act around him. But the kids were always good when they came up. If any one of them acted up, Lonnie just had to say one word to them and they immediately became angels. Lonnie didn't play with them; but he would always talk to them, and listen to them, just as he would with any adult. He commanded respect, and he gave it. He loved those kids; and they loved him.

Lonnie belonged to email discussion groups of blind people from around the country. One day he decided to offer his software engineering expertise to a new five-state consortium looking for help on their blind audio book project.

He spent many months on this project. He received very little financial compensation for his time; but he was grateful for the opportunity and enjoyed doing it. He was always generous with his time. He loved helping people.

Shortly after that project ended, he took on a project with a professor from the mid-west who was looking for software engineering help to train students at the Washington State School for the Blind, here in Washington state. Lonnie dedicated months on this project as well. When the project was ready to present to the school, and the students, the professor wanted Lonnie to come down to Vancouver, Washington, to tell the story of how he became a software engineer as a blind person. I drove us down to Vancouver, roughly a five-hour drive, for the presentation.

I asked Lonnie, on the morning he was to speak to the students, how he prepared for his speech. I said, "Really, Lonnie, most people prepare notes to have in-hand in case they're nervous and afraid they'll forget something. But you can't read your notes. So what will you do? And how do you keep from being nervous?" Lonnie's answer was "I just look into their eyes!" He was quite a joker too.

When he spoke to those blind students, I was never so proud of anyone in my life. He was a natural because that's who he was – an honest, humble man who truly wanted to help people. He brought tears to my eyes just listening to him.

I had heard Lonnie's story of how he became a software engineer many years before. He taught himself C++ by reading the book many times, with a magnifying glass – just before he became totally blind. He knew his sight was going and that he would need something to keep himself in the workplace. He had been an engineer in the telecommunications industry for many, many years. He knew that he could become a software engineer, so he taught himself.

I also learned over the years that if I ever got angry or upset with him for any reason, all I had to do was look in his eyes and I would immediately lose any anger I had. I would be calm. I felt like I was looking deep into his soul; and I would be at peace. Amazing experience! I've never experienced that with anyone else in my life and probably never will again. He could never see me; but I could feel so deeply connected to him when I looked into his eyes. He was truly an old soul.

Early in our marriage Lonnie decided to take advantage of the military benefits he had with the VA, so he signed up to go to the American Lake VA facility south of Seattle for blind rehabilitation training. He had to stay at the facility for two weeks, but he could come home on the weekend. I drove him down for his first week's stay and then went back to pick him up for the weekend, then back on Sunday to stay another week. It wasn't comfortable or easy for him; but he stuck it out. He had to go to Braille classes and give it a try, even though he had never tried it before in his life.

LONNIE

He said it was like taking a crash course in a foreign language; but he gave it his best. He was given a new computer to take home with him, which thrilled Lonnie. The instructors learned quickly that he could teach them a thing or two about using a computer. He was a brilliant software engineer. When we got home and set up his new computer in his office, he had a desk with two computers, one monitor and two back-up hard drives. His office looked like "command central". He was in computer heaven. He always had talking software on his computers. He could set the voice speed up so high on the computers that I couldn't understand a word, which amazed me.

Another big accomplishment for Lonnie was that he learned some new techniques on how to use his service cane. I learned a lot about that as well. It was a wonderful program. He had taken this blind rehab course maybe a year or so after we were married. Years later, he was given the chance to take a follow-up course with the VA as well.

Lonnie was excited about the opportunity to get new rehab information and opportunities from the VA since it had been many years since he had gone. He was always open to learning all he could. He was determined to be as independent as he could possibly be. The VA required Lonnie get a physical, including a chest X-Ray, to qualify for the program. I set up the physical appointment with our local primary care physician. When we were called by our PCP for a consultation a few days after the x-ray, I was concerned.

Our doctor, one of the sweetest, most caring young doctors we had ever met, called us back to discuss the fact that she saw spots on Lonnie's lungs that concerned her. She wanted to schedule him for further tests at the nearest hospital, in Mount Vernon. We did that. The radiologist stated that it was, most likely, just emphysema from smoking, and nothing to worry about. Our PCP disagreed and recommended we get a second opinion. She felt strongly about that. Thank God she did. We set up an appointment for Lonnie to be seen at the VA hospital in Seattle.

Lonnie was seen by the head of the Pulmonary department at the VA hospital in Seattle. He ordered a few more tests including a CT scan and MRI. The doctor was sure that it was lung cancer. With one more test, a PET scan, we were asked to see the pulmonologist for a consultation.

I called my step-daughter, Susan, and gave her the news. She and her husband, Tom, lived in Redmond, just east of Seattle. She and Mari came with us to meet with the doctor for the consultation and diagnosis. They both wanted to hear the diagnosis and support us as well. It was confirmed that he had Stage IV lung cancer. We were devastated. Lonnie was silent. He didn't even seem to wince when he heard the news. The doctor teared up as he told us. This doctor was the most compassionate, caring doctor we had ever met. I could not have imagined a doctor crying with the family as he gave his diagnosis, but he did.

LONNIE

No one said much of anything all the way home. We were in shock. Lonnie seemed very healthy for a seventy-one-year-old man. He had smoked for years and years but never even had a cough. I sat down on the bed that evening to talk with Lonnie about how we both felt and what we could do. He still didn't want to talk but was open to what I had to say. I said, "You're not saying much about this. How do you feel?" Lonnie said, "We've all got to die sometime." He wasn't being a smart aleck, just trying to make light of a situation that we knew we had no control over. He had never been one to talk about his emotions.

I couldn't help but cry, especially when as I sat there on the bed I remembered a "feeling" I had a few months earlier. The feeling came to me one day as I walked down the hallway of our house. It was a quick but strange feeling that I would be walking down this hallway one day in the empty house, by myself. I ignored it at the time, of course. Silly thought. I explained to Lonnie the "feeling" I had had months prior and how I didn't know how I could possibly live without him. What could he say?

Suddenly we had this unthinkable, terrifying reality in front of us. It stunned me. I'm sure it surprised him as well. It was shocking to know that he was going to die; and I had been given a premonition of this months earlier.

The doctor said Lonnie could try some chemo treatments but doubted this would do much good. The PET scan showed that the cancer had already spread to other organs, including his liver and brain. All we could do was let Lonnie live his last few months as happy and comfortable as possible.

The doctor arranged for Hospice to contact me so that we could have help taking care of Lonnie. I remembered my previous experience with Hospice, and the care they gave my mother and father before they died. I knew they would be angels; but the thought of having them help me take care of Lonnie made everything so real and final. The doctor wasn't sure how long Lonnie had to live. He guessed between a month and six months.

I decided to call Lonnie's two oldest daughters, Jannie and Terrie, who lived out of state. The older one lived in Iowa and the younger lived in California. He had not seen them in years. I had tried over the years to get Lonnie to call each one. He said, "They can call me if they want to talk to me." He was stubborn; but I persisted. I had gotten them connected on the phone a few years earlier and was so glad I had.

I knew a little bit of the story of how he and his two oldest girls had become estranged. When their mother and Lonnie divorced when both girls were very young, their mother moved to another state and no one kept in touch. I think the girls, and Lonnie, were glad that they had some time together before he got too ill.

They flew out in the first of September to see him. I had not met either girls in person before. They were incredible women; and I was so thrilled to meet them. They were both so loving and grateful to me for reconnecting them with their father, even if it was very late in his life.

Lonnie's two younger adult children, Susan and Justin who lived in Washington, came over as well, along with Mari and her three kids. Justin had married and had two young children, Samantha and Joshua. We didn't get to see them very often because he was in the process of a divorce and his wife would not allow him to have the kids, even for a day. It was very sad for the kids, and Justin; and we missed Lonnie's grandkids so much.

They all sat in Lonnie's room, on the bed and floor, and talked about great memories and special times with their dad. I tried to get Lonnie to describe in detail his work experience with NASA. He worked for NASA not long after he got out of the Navy. He had an amazing background in satellite communications, electronics and engineering. He had been involved in the Pacific Missile Tracking System and the Apollo Project. This was quite a legacy for Lonnie to leave his kids; and I wanted to record his description of what happened during these two projects with NASA. But he only made light of it all and barely described it. I didn't understand why he wouldn't say more.

Was he just humble?

It wasn't until a year or so after Lonnie passed away that I found out from his first wife that they had been married during his time with NASA and his drinking became a serious problem. Maybe that was it. I just found it so sad that he didn't share some of his experience in NASA with his kids. I have a document that was Lonnie's, from NASA, written by Astronaut Alan Shepard, Jr., in May of 1964. It's a fact sheet, by Shepard, with a description of the program, the lunar mission, blueprints and flow charts. It's incredible to read. This is one of the many treasures I have of Lonnie.

The day after the two girls left to go back home, Lonnie woke up in extreme pain. He said he just turned over on his side in bed and heard this loud 'pop' and was in immediate pain. I tried to get him into the car; but it was much too painful for him to move. I called 911 and an ambulance took him to the nearby hospital in Mount Vernon. This was just a temporary move on my part to get them to diagnose what caused his pain and to take him on to the VA hospital in Seattle.

I had been so dissatisfied with that hospital the first time Lonnie had gone there for a CT scan and lung biopsy. They were terrible. I couldn't wait for them to take an X-ray, tell us what had happened, and get him out of there. They took the X-ray and said they couldn't see anything. They helped me arrange for an ambulance to the Seattle VA and we were on our way.

When the VA took new X-rays, they determined immediately that he had a broken clavicle.

LONNIE

The doctor, the head of Pulmonology who had treated and diagnosed Lonnie, appeared in Lonnie's room to tell us that this broken clavicle probably occurred because the cancer was spreading to his bones. The doctor recommended that Lonnie have one radiation treatment, directed at his clavicle, just to keep the break to a minimum and alleviate some of Lonnie's pain. Lonnie had that treatment the next day; and I took Lonnie home to take care of him. This was in September.

I called Lonnie's daughters and son to let them know what had happened; I also called my sister and Mari. I spoke with Hospice to determine when they would be sending someone out to discuss their part in Lonnie's care. I arranged for a home healthcare company to deliver a hospital bed. My sister and brother- in-law, and my step-daughter and her husband, came up to help rearrange furniture so that we could have the hospital bed in Lonnie's room.

This is when it really hit me – that we would be taking care of Lonnie at home, until he died. It was beginning to feel too real and final to me. I knew the cancer had spread to other organs; but I also knew that when it spread to his bones, there probably wouldn't be much time left for Lonnie. I believe this is the time I went into autopilot to take care of him; I just didn't have time to feel the pain of losing him soon.

My step-daughter Susan took some time off from work, and so did my sister, Beth.

Justin, my step-son, promised to come and help me for the night shifts. Justin was still working and couldn't take time off from work during the day. He was also going through a difficult divorce. He was often not available at night when he said he'd be there but didn't show up or call. I'd take care of Lonnie, then, with sometimes only an hour or two of sleep in twenty-four hours, as he required medication for the pain every few hours. I learned later that Justin was having an incredibly hard time with his father's impending death and his own divorce; and he was drinking a lot.

It was a difficult time for all of us. Mari was working and couldn't take time off from work. I could also tell that she was having a difficult time facing Lonnie's illness and eventual death. No matter what feelings we had, there was nothing that we could do but make Lonnie feel comfortable before he died. That was my focus. I could see that Lonnie really gave up hope as soon as he heard the diagnosis. He didn't say much, ate maybe only a bite or two of food each day and was obviously depressed. I asked myself, "Would I feel any different?" I'm sure I would have given up hope as well.

Hospice helped more than I could even put into words. These people are truly angels on earth! Their most difficult task was to determine which drugs, and combination of drugs, would work best to make Lonnie comfortable.

LONNIE

This was hard. If he woke up moaning or talking strangely in his 'sleep', that meant he was in pain. If he woke up every two hours or so like that, he wasn't getting a strong enough dosage. Many times, he would call me into the room and ask me to do some things that were a part of his hallucinations. I went along with them just to make him happy since they were completely harmless. Hospice ended up trying so many combinations of drugs just to make Lonnie comfortable. And we found that Lonnie liked certain people from Hospice more than others, like the bed bath caregiver. She was cheery and caring. I could tell she brightened his day. Lonnie perked up, smiled and talked with her when she took care of him.

Most of the time, however, Lonnie was incoherent. When he was awake, he could only talk for a few minutes. I knew this was my only time to talk with him. All I could say was that I loved him; and I wanted him to know I would be ok. I felt strongly that he needed to know that before he died. I believe in reincarnation. I had read that when a loved one passes on, they will linger in a certain state – not go on to a higher consciousness – until they know that their loved one on earth will be ok. I believe that is why some people see their loved one at times after they've passed.

Lonnie had a couple of very good, long-time friends come to visit. One came all the way from Australia. He sat by Lonnie's bed for hours for a couple days. He talked with Lonnie, even though Lonnie didn't talk much.

This was the sign of a true friend. It warmed my heart that he loved Lonnie that much to come across the world to stay by his side before he passed.

We got the final diagnosis of Lonnie's stage IV lung cancer in August. Lonnie passed away three months later, on 11/12/11. Beth, Susan and I sat by Lonnie's bed for days watching his every breath, thinking each would be his last. I climbed into the hospital bed with Lonnie the night before he passed, because I wanted to hear his heart beat. I wanted to be close to him.

I had married this wonderful man late in my life. Lonnie was twelve years older than me. We had been together for thirteen years and married for twelve. I had finally found someone who loved me, and I loved him. We had a wonderful life together. Then it was gone. It seemed so impossible that he was gone. Time flew by way too fast. I cried on him for hours and then called the cremation company to take him. While waiting for them to come, I cut some hair from his grey ponytail for myself and for his kids and Mari. I also took out his diamond earring from his left ear that was a match to the one in my right ear, something that had been a symbolic connection of our shared love for each other for many years. It was so surreal to see the two men take him and I would no longer see him.

We had a wonderful memorial service for him just before Thanksgiving. Many friends and family came. Lonnie's younger brother came from Chehalis, Washington, the town where they both grew up.

LONNIE

Noel, Lonnie's brother, never left that city, living in the same house he had lived in all his life. Lonnie's two oldest daughters came from out of town. My niece Allison took my favorite photo of Lonnie and had it enlarged into a poster-sized photo of him that all could see at the service. She also put together the video of his life for me. I was so grateful for these gifts from her. I spoke at the service about what an incredible man Lonnie was. I don't know how I did it, but I know it came from my heart. A few of his friends spoke, hardly able to keep from breaking down. It was a wonderful celebration of him.

I tried to have a little Thanksgiving dinner for Mari, the grandkids and my step-children. It just didn't feel the same without Lonnie. We were trying to celebrate him, feel thankful for the time we had with him. I just felt numb. I was happy to have the family with me though.

Mari and her two older step-sisters went out one day before Lonnie's daughters had to go back home after the memorial service. When they returned, all three girls very proudly showed me the tattoos they had just gotten. Each one had the same tattoo, placed on each of their bodies in a different spot. The tattoos said, "Faith is seeing light with your heart when all your eyes see is darkness ahead." I had bought that plaque years before and placed it above Lonnie's dresser.

The girls all wore these words on their bodies to remind them of their Dad and what an amazing man he was. The girls would have this reminder of him on their bodies for the rest of their lives.

I would say that it took Mari a very long time to talk about Lonnie. He was one more person she became attached to and loved; and he was gone. She had loved him like a dad. He was firm, yet loving, with her. He never judged her. He advised her. And they had many years of talking alone, sitting outside on our back porch, smoking and drinking their beer – and contemplating the world.

CHAPTER 16

Alone

It wasn't until Lonnie passed away that I was able to truly grieve and feel the emptiness that I knew was coming. I had to take care of things while he was still alive. In fact, I had taken care of a lot in our marriage because he was blind. Maybe that didn't bother me so much because I was a type-A personality and loved being in control. I just knew what I had to do to keep him comfortable at the end. And I loved him so much.

It's amazing what our bodies and hearts can deal with in an urgent situation. It's like living in a world of adrenaline to handle what we must; and when it's really over, then we can fall apart. I had done this with Mari's life with me as well. I only allowed myself to fall apart after I took care of things. I had known in my mind that my life would be completely changed; but for some reason I also knew that I would be able to handle whatever came up. This time I felt really alone though. My parents were gone; Mari was unable to handle my grief because she couldn't handle her own. My sister Beth was the only one I could turn to, even though she could not totally relate to this grief because losing a spouse grief is so very different from losing parents grief.

I talked with Lonnie a lot while I was alone in our house. I knew that Lonnie would always look out for me. I felt his presence many times after he passed. I found coins sitting on tables, out of the clear blue, when we had never left money out anywhere in the house.

I took these coins as a sign of Lonnie taking care of me financially. I knew, because I handled the finances while we were married, that I would not be able to keep up the payments on our house. We had been living comfortably on Lonnie's pension and Social Security; but his pension would be gone after his death based on the annuity he had signed when he retired. He gave me messages through my 'other daughter', Lynn. In fact, one of the messages he sent me through Lynn was that I would write a book. He sent me messages of love through music when I was feeling such incredible grief.

I knew I would have to sell our home and move to an apartment and go back to work to have medical insurance. I had a layout, a vision board, of what I knew I had to do and what I envisioned it all looking like. For the first time in my life I was sure that I could do what I needed to do to pull myself up from the most difficult time in my life. Somehow, I just knew I could do it. The most painful time in my entire life became the most empowering. I'm not saying that I didn't fall apart. The grief would hit me in waves like I could never have anticipated. I just knew I would be ok. I knew the things I needed to survive would come. I finally had complete faith in God.

Thank God I had grief counseling, once a week, available to me through Hospice. Without Hospice, and the group of ladies I met who were all widowed around the same time I was, I could not have made it through my grief. But I know I became focused, while still grieving, because I had to handle certain issues quickly.

I had four critical things on my list of needs: sell my house and find an apartment I could afford; get a job so that I could have an income again; get medical insurance; and get healthy. As each one of these co-creations with God came to me, I knew I had discovered something new and powerful within me.

As I went through the worst experience of my life, losing my husband, Mari was there – but in the background. I saw her, and the kids; but that time after Lonnie's death seemed to be a blur. Mari and I would talk on the phone as often as we had in the past. But I was very focused on trying to pull myself up. And Mari was doing the same. I think Mari couldn't handle seeing me in pain. And that's quite serious to realize because that's how I had felt, for years - unable to handle her pain.

Mari had gotten completely out of the pharmacy field and was working in a women's retail clothing store; and she was doing quite well. She was raising her three amazing children still mostly by herself. They were turning into incredible young adults. Riley and Shea, the two oldest kids, were in high school; and Bentley, the youngest, was in middle school. All three seemed to have adapted so well to their shared custody arrangement with their parents.

I had needed to have my right hip replaced, due to years of arthritis, but had prolonged the surgery while I was taking care of Lonnie. Before I went back to work, I had the surgery done. I stayed with my sister, Beth, and Ross, my brother-in-law, to recuperate.

My sister even took some time off from work to take care of me. Beth's care for me after this surgery, along with her being by my side while Lonnie was dying, made me realize what an incredible sister I had. I don't know if I can ever repay the care and love she showed me in that year.

After I felt well enough to get out after the surgery, I went out to dinner one evening with Beth and Ross to meet some of their friends from their church. They were wonderful, friendly people who all expressed their condolences for my loss. But this was the first time I had been out since Lonnie had passed, and everyone at the dinner table was with their spouse, all couples. It hit me that I would no longer be a part of a couple; and it was very difficult to sit there and not cry. It hit me hard.

Mari had to work to support herself and the three kids, so I didn't get to see much of her while I recuperated for the next three months. But when I felt better, like a whole new person, I started eating very healthy – not a diet, just eating healthy. Lonnie and I had not eaten healthy for years and I had put on a lot of weight. I exercised about an hour every morning, took a job as a caregiver for an older couple which required a full day of barely sitting down at all, all day, and I felt fantastic. I started to lose weight. I went into the woman's clothing store where Mari worked and bought some new clothes for myself. I felt like a new woman! This was the first time since Lonnie had been ill that I did something for myself and felt proud of who I was becoming.

This good feeling was countered by the fact that I had put our house up for sale. It was difficult to face the fact that I was no longer going to live there. And each time I had to leave the house as the real estate agent showed it, I felt more depressed. Lonnie and I had lived there together for eight years, and I was there by myself after he died for nearly a year. When the house finally sold, I sat in the living room and sobbed. It was so final for me. So many memories were going to be left in that home.

I still hadn't found a new apartment by the time the house sold, so I was fortunate to be able to move into my friend Cheryl's home until I found one. It took about four months to find an apartment I could afford. It was an old house that had been turned into two apartments in north Everett, near the water side of the city. I had the upstairs apartment and a younger woman with teenage girls had the bottom apartment. It was charming. I loved it. I had a garage sale before I moved out of the house, knowing that I would be downsizing to an apartment. Then I put everything I owned into a storage unit until I found this apartment. Thank God for a moving company because I never could have moved the heavy furniture I had into that upstairs apartment!

Once I moved into the apartment, had the job that gave me an income and medical insurance, felt physically better than I had in probably twenty or thirty years, I decided to start dating.

After a year and a half of grieving and feeling empowered – all at the same time – I decided there was one more very important thing I needed in my life. That's when I joined an on-line dating service that my 'other daughter', Lynn, had recommended. I was just ready to share conversation with another man. It had been so long since I had dated, I felt like I was brand new at this dating thing. I wasn't sure what to do. I knew I wanted to meet someone with whom I could have a long-time, loving, spiritual relationship. I spent seven months dating a few men that I met on a reputable, on-line dating service, Match.com. I was picky. I got my hopes up in a few men, only to find I was just not finding the right one for me. No one I dated had the specific qualities I was looking for.

A dear friend gave me the greatest advice during this dating time in my life. She said, "If a man doesn't get you in the first five minutes of meeting him, he's not the one for you."
I took that to heart. I decided that if I truly wanted to spend the rest of my life with someone I loved, I needed to be very clear – as I was with my four other needs on my critical needs list – about what I wanted in this relationship. And then I trusted. This was also a new experience for me – to trust, when things might look strange, bad or even impossible. It was finally clear to me that if I let go of my expectations and trusted God and Lonnie to take care of me, I could have an even better situation appear than what I could visualize.

I was about to give up on this online dating process when I got a message from a man, Rand, on the site. He said he was just about to give up on the dating process when he noticed my profile and found me very interesting. He sounded very honest and genuine. Within a few days we talked and met. He lived only fifteen minutes away from me in Marysville. Rand had such a similar life situation: his wife had died a few years before Lonnie had, of Stage IV lung cancer as well. We bonded so quickly and, yet, took our time and were cautious.

On our first date, Rand brought me flowers and a book by C.S. Lewis, "A Grief Observed." I found the gift of the book to be so thoughtful, so touching. He took us to lunch at Ray's Boathouse in Seattle, then drove around his old neighborhood where he had grown up. He was so easy to talk to; and we discovered that we had lived in some of the same suburb cities of Seattle as well. I felt like we had known each other for years. It was the beginning of the most romantic, loving relationship I had ever experienced. I thought that I could never expect to meet someone who could love me more than Lonnie had, or that I could never love someone as much as I had loved him, but my relationship with Rand surpassed all expectations. We spent every possible moment together that we could. I was able to shift my work schedule so that I worked only Monday through Wednesday every week, giving us a four-day weekend all the time. We were in heaven.

We had started dating in July and by February of the next year Rand had asked me to move into his house with him. The lease on my apartment was up then, so it was perfect timing. He lived in a gorgeous neighborhood on a hill with a view of the water. It was a little awkward for me at first because he knew all his neighbors and the neighbors had all known his late wife. But once he introduced me to his neighbors, they were wonderful and happy for both of us. They eventually became great friends of mine as well.

Rand and I had so much in common, including our OCD'ness. It took a while for us to work through that process. He was a meticulous housekeeper; and so was I. We both loved decorating and gardening. Rand and his late wife had designed the home, had it custom built and landscaped their home beautifully.

The mature landscaping was gorgeous. We loved working in the yard and maintaining that beautiful corner lot of ours. One of the neighbor's little granddaughter called our home "the park". Rand made me feel like this was my home too.

Mari and the kids came over as often as they could after I moved into Rand's home. They lived about a half hour from us. The kids were in awe of the home. It was really a mansion compared to what they had seen in the past. But Rand always made them feel comfortable. And they were. We tried to take the kids to things they had never been to before, like the state fair.

We took them out to dinner to nice restaurants when we could. Rand also loved playing football and baseball with Bentley. Both Rand and Bentley were good at sports. Rand was an awesome man to my daughter and grandkids.

While Mari was in a relationship with a man, and was happy, she was not so concerned that she and I had infrequent conversations, even when I was in a relationship. But if her relationship was not good, or ended completely, then she seemed a little upset with me. She acted like I ignored her. It seemed she needed me more then. It also seemed to me that she was not happy for me during this time, like she felt, "how can you have two very happy relationships so late in life and I can't even have one?" And she seemed to drink more. There were times when I found out from the kids that she had been so drunk that she passed out – in the kitchen, or on the front porch, and really hurt herself. I was just glad she'd been at home! When I talked to her about this she said, "Yeah, I know Mom." She still had never been to an AA meeting and refused to go to one. She would sometimes quit drinking for a short time, and then go right back to it. The kids were pretty concerned about her. Her psych counselor was as well. But no one could get her to stop drinking.

She had a secretive relationship with a man for about a year. They would drink together, so giving up drinking during this time was certainly not an option.

One night, after drinking for quite a while, she decided to drive to his house. He had always come to her house. She didn't really know exactly where he lived; she just had a general idea of the neighborhood. She drove around the neighborhood, couldn't find the house and pulled over on one of the residential streets and passed out in the car. She was very lucky that she encountered a very kind and generous policeman who drove her home that night, without even giving her a ticket. I had to drive her around the neighborhood the next day where she "thought she had been" the night before so we could find her car before it could be towed away. I emphasized with her that she was SO LUCKY. She could have been in an accident, killed someone or herself, or even could have been taken to jail with a DUI. What could I do with her, or for her, to get her to realize how serious her drinking had become? I knew her drinking was at a critical point. I remember her saying then that she realized how lucky she was and that she "saw this as a sign to quit drinking."

I think that's when I realized all the talking, lecturing, counseling, etc. could not help her unless Mari was ready to help herself. The kids couldn't take responsibility for her and neither could I. She couldn't either.

I had seen her over the years go from drinking, to stopping and eating well, and then back to drinking. It seemed each time she drank it was when she felt her life was not going the way she wanted it to. She felt she had no control. She had some pretty good jobs, but nothing that made her feel like she was contributing something to the world, or even to herself. Even though she had been in counseling for years and years, and had also been on antidepressants for that long, I knew Mari did not feel she deserved the best in life. And that was true for her love life as well. I could tell by the way she talked to me and acted that she just wasn't happy and didn't know how to help herself.

Chapter 17

Our Wedding(s)

Rand and I were happier than we could have ever imagined. Mari still struggled between drinking and sobriety and finding a job that could pay her enough to support her and her three teenagers. She was making it; but I could tell that she was not happy. She dated here and there. I don't think, however, that there was anyone she was serious about.

In April Rand asked me to marry him. We picked out our rings and then went up to Bellingham, to one of the parks by the water, so that Rand could officially ask me to marry him. He was so romantic that when we got our rings after they had been made and sized, he planned with the wait staff at Canlis to have the ring served with our dessert. Canlis is just about the most elegant restaurant in Seattle. I had never been there until this momentous evening. That made three times that he asked me to marry him.

We set the date for August of that year. It would turn out to be thirteen months after our first date that we would get married. We were so excited. We decided to have the wedding at our house. We had such a beautiful home; and the backyard was perfect for our ceremony, especially after we bought a pergola and put it up in the backyard. We were able to train our gorgeous Wisteria to grow over the pergola in time for the wedding. We spent a great deal of time and care in making our landscaping even more beautiful.

OUR WEDDING(S)

We planned our wedding together. We asked Mari to be our maid of honor, and Riley to give me away. Dawn, my best friend from grade school, and Lynn, my 'other daughter', both planned to come. We were so excited.

Mari, just a little over a week before our wedding, called me with a shocking story. She was in the hospital. She had developed a kidney infection that had not gotten any better with the normal antibiotics. She ended up staying in the hospital for five days. The doctors found the right strength of antibiotics to stop the infection just before her body developed Sepsis. Scary! Rand and I went to see her while she was in the hospital. We took the grandkids as well so that they could see their mom. We knew they were as worried about her as I was. She was close to having this infection take over her other organs. They allowed her to leave the hospital with an IV antibiotic that she could maintain on her own because of her pharmacy experience with IVs. She did very well in our wedding, with an IV port in her arm. She looked good, but tired. No one knew that she had just gotten out of the hospital after such a difficult ordeal, except when she told them. We were so relieved that she was feeling better and could attend. Rand and I were thrilled that she was in our wedding; and I think Mari was too.

Our wedding was beautiful. All our family and friends were there, including our neighborhood friends. The weather was just perfect – not too hot for an August day.

Our ceremony was held in the pergola, with rental chairs lined up in rows for our guests to witness our happy event. Then we rearranged the chairs and tables for everyone to get their food in the house and bring it outside to enjoy each other's company and great weather. It couldn't have turned out to be a better wedding. I was so proud of Mari and how great she looked, considering her recuperation from such a serious illness. The grandkids were beautiful and happy. I was especially proud of Riley walking me down the aisle to meet Rand at the pergola for our ceremony.

The next morning, we took Dawn and Lynn out to breakfast before they had to leave to go back home. Then Rand and I left for our honeymoon to the San Juan Islands and Victoria, B.C. We were so excited! We had a wonderful week. We were so blissfully happy.

After we returned from our honeymoon, we decided to do a little more interior decorating in our home. We had a large transom window opening above the double doors to our office, right off the large entryway, that had no glass in it. To have a large stained glass, or etched glass, window installed would have cost a fortune. We decided to add a clear piece of glass in the framed-out transom opening and add a beautiful piece of glass film on the window. We were excited about our clever idea. We just needed someone to help Rand install that piece of glass.

It just so happened that Mari was dating a long-time guy friend at that time. They had just been friends for over eight years; but they had always had an attraction for each other.

Their life circumstances had just not allowed them to get together until then; they had both been in other relationships in the past. Mari brought Rick, this long-time friend, over one day to help Rand install the transom glass. I hadn't seen him in years either, so I wasn't quite sure what to expect. I had seen him a few times when they got together in the past and I just remembered him being such a wonderful guy. He was friendly, polite and an all-around nice guy. He had a son that he was solely responsible for since his ex-wife had left them; and his son had medical issues. I was impressed with how he seemed to be such a good father. I could never understand why he and Mari hadn't gotten together sooner.

Rick was very helpful but there was something about him that day that Rand and I couldn't put our fingers on. He seemed different than what I had remembered him being. He talked a lot, like he was extremely hyper. He made Rand nervous. It seemed like Rick was on drugs.

Rick and Mari spent a lot of time together. The kids were even excited to see them together. They really liked him. But time showed Rick's new, true nature. It turned out years past, when he and Mari didn't have as much contact with each other, that Rick had become seriously injured on a construction job. He had injured his neck, requiring surgery. He then became addicted to opioid pain killers. And, as I learned over time from Mari, Rick also became addicted to meth.

This explained why he was so hyper. He was quite a mess. I was afraid for Mari and the kids and strongly told her so. I had heard horror stories about meth and I was sure this could be disastrous for Mari and the kids. I could not comprehend how she thought she could "work through" this situation. This drugging was not something she could get Rick to stop – just by loving him. I knew she loved Rick; but I knew she was not going to be happy with him.

While we discovered this about Rick, he and Mari became engaged. She said she was happy and was sure that she and Rick could work this out. I thought this was an insane idea! Rick asked us to help him plan an evening dinner at a nice restaurant, with the kids and ourselves, so that he could propose to Mari officially. Rick was truly beside himself. We knew he loved Mari.

I was learning where to have boundaries with Mari, so we left her to work out (or not) her relationship with Rick and their engagement. She was determined to try to make it work. There wasn't much Rand and I could say to her and we knew that Mari would not listen to us. We thought this was such a ridiculous idea. I felt Mari had essentially lost her mind. I tried to talk with her about what an unsafe relationship this would be, with her drinking and Rick's drugging. She'd say, "Yeah I know Mom. We'll get him into a treatment program." We couldn't picture a wedding for them. And we were praying for nothing to go seriously wrong.

CHAPTER 18

Retirement

Rand was such an incredible planner, organizer and caretaker of the budget that he helped me plan the date I could finally retire when I was 64. Through a caregiving agency I had been taking care of an elderly couple for nearly three years; and it was really wearing me out. Even though I only took care of them three days a week, their needs – and the family requests for their care – became more and more demanding. I had to feed them, bathe them, take them to doctor appointments, grocery shop and help them with their aches and pains. I loved them dearly, but it was like taking care of two toddlers. I was so stressed. One day I called Rand from work to pick me up from the couple's home and take me to the hospital. I was sure I was having a heart attack. It turned out to be stress, nothing heart related. I loved the couple; but I was just maxed out.

I felt so relieved and excited when I could officially say I was retired. I felt like Rand saved my life. I was thrilled. Rand had been retired for years. He'd retired just before his late wife had passed away so that he could take care of her. Rand planned a big surprise family get-together at one of our favorite restaurants in Edmonds to celebrate my retirement. It was so awesome. And I felt so blessed.

We finally had the freedom to go where we wanted, when we wanted. We loved taking trips to Canada, the coast of Oregon (especially Cannon Beach) and even just day trips.

We talked about going to Hawaii, since Rand had never been there. We planned an anniversary trip to Maui, a little later than our anniversary date, so that my sister and brother-in-law, Beth and Ross, could go with us. It was an anniversary celebration for both couples, as Beth and Ross were married 30 years and we were one year.

I had a friend that I had known since Mari was little who owned a condo we could rent for two weeks, in Kihei. It was hot there, much hotter than we expected for November. But we had a wonderful time and spent a lot of time on the beach, in the ocean and in the condo pool. We drove around the island, checking out every view and restaurant we could possibly find. We also took a helicopter ride, getting the most incredible views of the island. We took a dinner cruise one evening. We did some snorkeling off a cruise boat one day. We loved it so much there, we listened to a sales pitch about buying a time-share condo. Rand and I signed up for the condo, thinking that this would be a good way to come often to Hawaii and travel around the world and visit some of the countries we'd like to see. We were guaranteed by the salesman and his supervisor that we would have enough points to travel to three different places around the world. The airfare was to be covered by the number of points they were giving us.

RETIREMENT

None of the promises of points and trips turned out to be what they guaranteed. We got out of the condo within a year, without even taking one trip. Most people would have said, "I told you so." Luckily no one did. It was a learning experience for Rand and me. We would never fall for something like this again. We knew if we ever wanted to take a trip across the world, we'd just do it and stay in a hotel or rent someone's condo.

Rand and I talked about selling our big house and downsizing. We were both a little torn about this since we had such a gorgeous home. We really didn't need the space, so we figured we could buy a smaller home and have a smaller mortgage. We looked and looked, meeting with real estate agents, thinking that a condo might be the option for us. What we looked at initially was not impressing us enough to move.

We decided to contact an agent in Bellingham, which was about fifty miles north, and look there. We had already taken day trips up there, even got engaged for the first time in Bellingham. It had everything we could want in a city: old and new areas in which to live; beautiful mountain ranges and Mount Baker views from almost everywhere; waterfront parks; and the people seemed very nice, with a lot of social views with which we agreed. We put our house up for sale and found a new solar development that we knew we would love. The home we chose was nearly one-half the size of our existing home, very modern, with a much smaller lot. And we could watch the new home being built.

We prepared for the downsizing, putting a lot of things, and some furniture, into our 3-car garage for a garage sale. We spent a week preparing for the garage sale. It turned out to be the most profitable sale we'd ever had. What we didn't sell, we gave to kids, grandkids and charity. We gave Rand's beautiful baby grand piano to his stepdaughter. I knew it was difficult for him to let it go; but we knew we wouldn't have enough room in our smaller new house for it. He made quite a few sacrifices for us, like also selling his prized 1958 Corvette and his Chrysler 300C.

Our new home wasn't ready when our house sold, so we had to put our furniture and things we decided to keep into one of our neighbor's huge RV garage, and another neighbor's garage with the things we would be giving to Mari. We were so incredibly grateful to the neighbors for the use of their garages, especially since we couldn't find a storage unit anywhere. All storage unit locations were full; no one had available space between Marysville and Bellingham.

We moved into Mari's house for a month and a half until the house was ready. Bentley let us take over his room and bathroom. We got along super and enjoyed our time together before our big move. Mari and the kids were going to be moving to Mill Creek a day after we would move. As soon as we all moved in opposite directions, we'd live about one and a half hours apart, fifty miles or so. Our time together was valuable.

RETIREMENT

The two youngest kids were busy with homework and school activities, and Riley was working, so we didn't get to see a lot of them. But when we did, we treasured the time we had with them. They were growing up so fast. Riley had graduated from high school the year before. Shea was a junior in high school and Bentley was in his last year of middle school. We celebrated Bentley's fourteenth birthday while we were staying with them. It was amazing to think that Mari's baby, Bentley, would be a freshman in high school the following year. They were so fun to be around especially when they'd all get silly and laugh like crazy. We loved them dearly.

Rand and I fixed dinner for everyone most days and helped Mari pack her things while she and the kids were at work and school. Rick wasn't around much, thank heavens. Rand and I tried not to judge him; but we weren't very tolerant of his "hyper" behavior and neither were the kids.

It was sad to leave our big, beautiful home. But when we moved into our new home, we were so thrilled – and very much surprised – to find that we could be very comfortable in our new space, even if it was almost one-half the size of our home we just sold. It was a beautiful, new, modern solar home. And we had a little bit of a backyard that Rand and I could landscape. We loved our new home, the neighborhood and Bellingham. We felt very strongly that Bellingham would be a great new place for Rand and me to grow our spirituality as well. It surpassed our expectations. We met so many wonderful, spiritual friends when we moved here.

CHAPTER 19

Happiness for Mari?

We hoped that Mari and Rick could work out their relationship. We wanted to see her happy and stable. We urged her to convince Rick to go to couples counseling. However, Rick became so difficult to live with, so aggressive and obsessive in his need for her, Mari had to give up her ring, have him move out and eventually get a restraining order against him. It was a very ugly situation. It was Mari's first exposure to a stalker! He just wouldn't leave her alone. He was obsessed with her. She had to get a restraining order to keep him away. She moved to Mill Creek right after we moved to Bellingham, so Rick didn't know where she lived, thank God.

This was extremely devastating for Mari. She had known Rick for years. He had never acted this way in the past. And she had never known anyone on drugs. Neither had we. This situation was way beyond them trying to work it out because they loved each other. She knew what kind of a man he had been; and she hoped that their love could help him. But she learned it could not. It seemed to fuel his scary behavior. She knew they had loved each other for years. It was difficult for her to face the fact that he could not be the same person she had known.

It was sad for everyone around Mari to see someone who really was a kind and generous person – someone who could, under healthy circumstances, be a wonderful husband for Mari – be so messed up.

We felt sorry for him but knew he needed to stay away from Mari and the kids until he got help. Those drugs affected Rick's behavior and made him horrible to be around. They made Mari's drinking look normal, even though that certainly wasn't the case. Luckily for Mari and the kids, she realized that there was no way she could ever have a healthy relationship with Rick.

He just wouldn't leave her alone. He kept calling and texting her constantly. Mari had to threaten Rick with calling the police since the restraining order was in effect. Mari was a wreck. When I talked with her on the phone she told me all about all the constant calls and texts. I could tell she was so stressed. She knew she had to report this to the police to get him to stop, even though she still loved him and felt badly for how his life was deteriorating. Because of his random stalking, she never felt safe. In fact, Mari had been a caregiver, for over a year, for a wonderful lady who had been dying of cancer. Mari became very attached to her, as the woman reminded Mari of her grandmother, my mother. When this woman died, Rand and I met Mari at the funeral to support her. As we sat next to Mari in the back row of the church, we were extremely shocked to find Rick suddenly standing behind Mari. Mari jumped and was afraid. I gasped. He said he wanted to "be there for her" since he knew she had become very attached to this wonderful grandmother-like person. This horrified Mari. She had a restraining order against him and he suddenly appeared at this funeral. How did he even know about this?

It was creepy. The sons of the woman who died, who knew Mari very well since she had been taking care of their mother for a long time, asked her if they needed to ask Rick to leave. Mari said yes. The sons were standing in the back of the church when they saw Rick come up behind Mari and upset her. It was such a weird incident, almost like watching a movie – where you knew the guy was in love with the woman he was stalking, and you couldn't help but feel sorry for him, even as he scared us with his obsession. Rick had taken a bus, walked in the rain to the funeral, and had to find a way home. As she was trying to get over Rick and the hurt she had experienced in this relationship, Mari felt like she had to look over her shoulder or watch her phone constantly – and didn't have much time to heal. Her counselor was a life saver.

Once Rick was out of her life Mari seemed to be ok, although her drinking picked up again. I would hear about her drinking, not from Mari but from the kids. They had cell phones; and Shea, especially, would call me to say that she was upset about her mom drinking and asked, "Will you please talk to your daughter about her drinking?" I got on the phone with Mari and said, "You know you have to stop drinking, Mari. You are scaring the kids. You could get hurt and they should not have to be the ones worrying about you." She said, like she always did, "Yes, I know Mom."

Rick contacted Mari a year later, stating that he had spent a long time in rehab in Montana. He wanted to see her and explain how sorry he was and have her see how well he was doing. We didn't know this until a few months after they met again. Mari had been afraid to tell Rand and me because she knew we would be furious that she even considered letting him back into her life at all. She had gone through such hell with him, and then the ugly breakup and stalking. We just couldn't comprehend how she could even risk going through the pain all over again. Mari's counselor felt this as well and said, "You know if you have another breakup with him, you may not recover this time."

We found out that they were trying to make it work again just before Thanksgiving. We always got together with Mari and the kids, either at our house or hers, for special holidays and birthdays. But when she explained that she and Rick were back together, Rand and I both said there was absolutely no way that we would be in the same room with him again. Rick was toxic. It was like he took all the air out of the room! We loved Mari and the kids; and we just couldn't stand seeing them exposed, all over again, to such toxicity. I was so afraid for her mental and emotional welfare, not to mention her physical welfare since he had stalked her.

Knowing how important that holiday was to all of us, Mari got Rick to go somewhere else for Thanksgiving.

We had a great dinner at Mari's apartment. We loved being around the kids. Another year had gone by and Riley was nearly 21 and working; Shea was a freshman at the University of Washington; and Bentley was a freshman in high school excelling in sports and academics. They were so grown up now! And our time with them was so precious.

After they got back together, Mari and I didn't talk on the phone often while Rick was there. I guess I just didn't want to know about it not working out between them, of which I was sure. I had a gut feeling they could not be happy together. Unless they went to major couple's counseling, which they didn't, their relationship would be like oil and water. And it was.

We planned to go to Mari's for Christmas. We had to be with Mari and the kids for Christmas. We just had to work out when – Christmas Eve or Christmas day – based on when Rick would be there. We asked Mari if Rick would be gone at any time during those two days. We usually spent the night at her place, so we wouldn't have to drive home in the dark and snow. We spent Christmas Eve day at her house and then the night at a nearby hotel, so that Mari and Rick could spend Christmas together as well. We just couldn't be around him for very long. But Rick was ok this time. He wasn't extremely hyper. And he was very generous to Mari and the kids. He even helped Mari buy some of our gifts. Rick was really a likeable guy when he was calm. And, again, I realized how I felt terrible that it couldn't work out for them.

HAPPINESS FOR MARI?

I just knew that his drinking and drugging personality was poison to Mari's drinking personality, which was sad for both of them. We all wanted them to be happy.

But as time went on, shortly after Christmas, Rick was back to his crazy behavior. This time Mari didn't feel the emotional pain she had when they first broke up. She had had enough. He was driving her nuts. And she didn't like how she was truly disliking him. She had him leave, saying that there was absolutely no way they could ever be together. She was adamant.

I could tell there was a difference in Mari's view of Rick this time. She was truly done. She didn't feel sad or guilty this time. She had enough. And she said she wanted some time alone, with no plans for any other relationship, for a while. She wanted to regroup. I was so very proud of her. She got out in time. She still had her sanity and health.

CHAPTER 20

Her Dad's Family

Mari's grandmother on her father's side had lived in Oklahoma for as many years as we had lived in the Seattle area. Mom, as I called her, had moved there with her two youngest children to be near her family a few years after she and Allen's dad divorced. Mom's family, most of her sisters and her mom, still lived there; and she had no real reason to stay in Arizona any longer.

Mom dated an old friend in the little town where she lived; and they married. One of the couple times that Mari and I flew to visit Mom, we were able to get to know Mom's wonderful new husband, Leroy. It was so great to see Mom happy. Leroy was great for Mom. They were married for quite a few years until, one day, Leroy had a massive heart attack while driving his car and died. We knew this was devastating for Mom. Mari and I couldn't make it to Leroy's funeral. Again, I missed being there for Mom when she lost someone so close to her. I hadn't been able to go to her son Harold's funeral when he had been killed many years before. I was able to make it to see her a few times in the years following. I made sure I talked with her on the phone often. She was so very special to Mari and me.

Mom's youngest daughter, Regina, was always there for her. Regina took on all care and responsibilities for Mom. I think everyone, including Mom's own sisters who lived in nearby cities, felt Mom was in such good hands with Regina that they never offered to help.

This became particularly apparent when Mom developed Alzheimer's. This was very tough for Regina, but she never complained. Regina took such amazing care of Mom, even to her dying day.

Rand and I couldn't afford to go to Mom's funeral; but Mari was able to go with the help of Lynn, my 'other daughter', her best friend who now lived in Dallas. Mari was so grateful to spend some time with her black side of the family, celebrating her grandma. This was very important to her. Her grandma had been so important to her. She loved her. The only thing Mari regretted was that she had not spent enough time with her over the years. Once Mari became a mom herself, it was very difficult for her to get away. But Mari felt good about reconnecting with her other side at the funeral.

Only months later, we got a call from Regina saying that her youngest brother, Mari's Uncle Fritz, was dying of colon cancer and may not live much longer. Fritz was only a year and a half older than Mari. Regina also took care of Fritz and his affairs. Regina was such an incredibly strong woman. I don't know if I could have handled this just after handling my mother's death, as she did. I could not go to Fritz's funeral because Rand was having some serious heart issues and I could not leave him alone. We paid for Mari to go to the funeral. This was so important to her. This time she explained, after coming home from the funeral, that she felt like she had only one person left on her dad's side of the family now, her Aunt Regina.

Mari's dad did not come to either his mom's or his brother's funerals.

Mari experienced a lot of grief after losing her grandmother and uncle all in one year. She decided to reach out to her dad through Facebook. She had not heard one word from her dad or half-sister in at least ten years. This turned out to be such an unexpected, painful disaster for Mari. Her dad said, "It's been both our faults for not staying in touch." Mari replied with, "What happened to your promises to stay in touch?" Then Mari's half-sister popped in with some nasty comments on Facebook saying, "How dare you talk to MY dad that way?" It was stupid, hateful and ugly. And it nearly killed Mari again. I could see that Mari was so completely devastated. She was rejected, one more time, by her father and his new family. I told Mari, as did her counselor, that this was a sign for Mari to write off her father, as difficult as that would be. He was never going to be there for her. She needed to face that fact. I think this hurt Mari to the core – again.

CHAPTER 21

It's Not Over

It's never over when you're a parent. Just when I thought Mari was healing and doing so well with her breakup with Rick for roughly six months, she announced to me that they got back together, and had been for a few months. She was afraid to tell me because she was sure I would be angry at her, or disappointed. That made three times that they tried to make it work. The second time they got back together, it was because Rick explained to Mari that he had gone to rehab and was completely off drugs. However, after they got back together, Mari realized that he was drinking in place of the drugs. Rick was still a mess. This time, Rick stopped drinking and Mari believed he was the "old Rick" she used to know many years ago. It turned out Rick was not the old Rick, even sober. He was still controlling and volatile.

Mari thought that I was mad about them getting back together. I explained to her that I was not. I was just disappointed that she had done this again. I was worried for her. I told her that I only wanted them to be happy, whether together or not. But I felt that if Rick stopped drinking, and Mari did not (which she said she did not), then Mari was not being fair to Rick, and could be tempting him to drink. And she was not the healthy person she needed to be for him. They both needed to be completely free of any drugs or alcohol to have a healthy relationship. I only hoped that they saw that so as not to destroy themselves.

I believe Mari, finally, saw how critical it was to be absolutely committed to being alcohol free - to love herself, to be able to love someone else in a healthy relationship – to be happy. She had cut down her drinking while Rick had been there; but didn't quit completely. I wish them all the love and happiness in the world, living apart.

She ended the relationship again – finally – and is feeling much better about herself. She's still drinking at times and looking for a new love relationship. I wish she'd give herself a little more time before jumping into another. She has an exciting new job, working for a company that is new to the Pacific Northwest; and I am thrilled to see how happy she is right now! God, I hope so. Please let this be her moment to shine!

CHAPTER 22

What's the Answer?

Mari seemed to be happy after ending her relationship with Rick for good. I could tell she was proud of herself this time. I felt she was getting back on her feet, emotionally and financially. I was concerned, however, about telling her I wanted to write this book.

I was so afraid that she would be very upset and say, "No way, Mom!" But she surprised me. She said, "It's funny that you would say that because I've been thinking about writing a book myself." Wow! Maybe someday she will write her memoir – her version of our life together. I hope it will be as cathartic for her as it has been for me. I explained to her that I would consult with her on everything I wanted to write about, especially comparing what she remembered with what I remembered. She's been very open and honest about her life with me now.

Mari had a fear of dying most of her life. She was sure she would not live to be twenty-one. I knew about Mari's fear of dying. She was obsessed with death. All I could say was, "No, Mari, you're not going to die. You'll have a good, long life. I think everyone, at some time in their lives, believes that they will die young; but they don't." Her fears could have come from the fact that she witnessed two car accidents when she was young, including the one in the mountain pass with my mom, that made her realize that people close to her came close to death.

She was sure that these two accidents, and my brother-in-law's death, were signs that she was going to die. She was there when my parents took their last breaths. She was more afraid of death than I had ever known. I'd like Mari to see that I've also experienced the pain of losing those I've loved the most. This is the nature of life. We're born; we learn to live our lives as good, healthy, loving beings; and we die. Maybe her fear of dying came from her insecurity, abandonment and shame, or could have even come from a past life she lived. Maybe that's also a part of what made her want to die. I don't know. She can't explain it either.

While writing this book, I felt myself avoiding an issue about the relationship between Mari and me - because I was concerned that my readers might not accept this subject. I know, as a deep-rooted gut feeling and through many past life psychic readings, that Mari and I had a terrible past life together. It was not a mother/daughter relationship in that lifetime; it was a male/female relationship. And I know that she murdered me in that lifetime. Tough one. And just as sure as I know this fact, I also know that our difficult relationship in this lifetime is because we are trying to work out this karmic damage. We must work out our relationship this time.

There were also some traumatic things I really did not know about, including some secrets Mari kept from me, until she gave me a timeline of the events she remembered – particularly that she was a little too wild even in grade school, with some inappropriate touching, after she had been raped by her cousin at age four.

WHAT'S THE ANSWER?

It became a big part of her life; and I didn't realize it until she became pregnant at age fifteen. I found out she was pregnant only because she was very ill and had to tell me. She kept these events from me because she was ashamed and never knew how to tell me; and she was terrified to tell me because she was afraid I would abandon her like her father had.

She has lived with shame and guilt all her life. All the things that have caused her to feel guilt and shame - and abandonment by her father - are at the core of her pain and they have left traumatic scars. That's why I have called these things traumas.

As I've gotten older, I've realized I made some mistakes in raising my child. I felt like I let her down because I wasn't there to protect her at times when she was being abused. I read recently that there is no greater trauma than to be hurt by people we count on to support and protect us. This sentence hit me to the core of my soul.

There's also an honest fact I needed to face about myself: sometimes I just didn't want to know – I couldn't handle Mari being in pain. If I knew she was in pain, I would have to face my pain about it. I felt helpless, yet responsible. I needed to face my own fear of pain. I just realized these facts as I was writing this book. I kept these feelings deep down inside me, hoping I'd never have to face them.

I've needed to move toward that pain to grow and help my daughter grow. That's my spiritual path. That's what I'm here for. I've needed to help both of us face our pain.

I feared talking about this pain could be unbearable, like maybe I would take on her pain even more and it would consume me. I've been afraid it would destroy our relationship. In fact, not talking about our pain has affected our relationship negatively. I thought it would make me vulnerable and show my flaws as a mother, which would make me imperfect. But isn't she worth me taking the chance? It shouldn't be so difficult to talk with Mari. In the rest of my life I'm a talker, a "confronter" and I need to settle things.

Only recently have I confronted our pain. I believe that Mari has blamed me for what happened to her, especially as she got older; and I took that blame and responsibility to heart. I've not had a heart-to-heart conversation with her, just showing up - getting out of my own way, not worrying about what to say - just being there for her and loving her. I've sensed the tension between us over the years; and I need to face this with Mari. I learned, when Mari attempted suicide for the first time, how critical compassion is for both of us. I need to be more compassionate – and God knows my daughter should be the number one person for whom I should be showing compassion.

I realized for the first time while writing this book that one of the reasons I didn't fall apart each time Mari attempted suicide was because I couldn't afford to. I was the only parent she had, and I had to keep our lives together. I had to make our lives as stable as possible. I had to be the rock for Mari. I had to work.

WHAT'S THE ANSWER?

I had to show her love and try to help her get back on her feet, even when I didn't really know how.

I've also read that there is no good or bad parent – only a present parent. So was I always present for Mari? Was I there when she needed me? I'm not really sure. Can a parent ever be sure? I tried to be, even if I couldn't always be there in ways she wanted or needed every time. I listened to her and was an outlet, even when I had no idea what to say to her to make her feel any better. Sometimes that was all I could do. There were also times when Mari was living a good life as an adult and didn't contact me unless she was upset and "needed her mom". Sometimes she got busy with her life before kids, and then certainly with kids, and just didn't talk to me as often.

I grappled with guilt and confusion. Did she want me to feel guilty for not being there whenever she needed me, dropping what was going on in my life, because she was so upset at the time, especially when I had extra responsibilities with Lonnie or when we were dealing with possible open-heart surgery for Rand? Sometimes it seemed an unreasonable demand. She was an adult, with her own kids. The issues were always the same – she was unhappy with something in her life – and no matter what I said or did, I could not change anything for her. She had to do that. I tried to tell her that many times; but she was not ready to hear it.

So where is the line between what I could do and what my child could do to help herself? I tried to lead Mari to things that I thought could help her feel better. I tried to lead by example, even though she saw that I didn't make good choices in my own personal relationships and marriages until I was forty-seven years old. Maybe it would help Mari if I admitted that I've made mistakes that could have made me feel terrible about myself. But I have not felt that way because I've realized that mistakes make us better, stronger - by learning from our mistakes – not by beating ourselves up for them. That's something that I've felt confident in most of my life and I had these beliefs confirmed when I went through the "Excellence Series" in Seattle when Mari was a teenager. I've stayed positive and focused on becoming a person who loves who I am and deserves to be loved as that person. I don't think Mari gets that yet. I think she's trying, but just hasn't totally gotten it yet.

I've struggled also with when does my parenting come in, or end, and my child's choices begin? I read an article recently that said, "We may think that being a good parent has to do with controlling our children's achievement or behavior; but it really comes down to accepting the fact that the only person's behavior we can really control is our own." It also stated, "Hopefully, this humbling realization comes relatively soon in the relationship between parent and child so that parents can work on the baggage that they're still carrying from their own childhood and not pass it on for the next generation."

WHAT'S THE ANSWER?

As to carrying my childhood into my parenting, I thought I had a very healthy, loving childhood. I went through a few years of counseling myself. I didn't experience trauma like my daughter did. I was just not happy with my life at that time. I felt I needed help. I struggled, in my twenties as a single mom, with guilt and anger and felt my mother was somewhat responsible for my lack of love and affection. How's that for warped?! She was so caring and loving; but she was also very tough, and selective in giving out compliments and hugs. I remember times in my childhood when I wanted hugs, to be held, and I didn't get that affection. I also felt she was judgmental.

I told my mother how I felt she was responsible for my lack of affection. It devastated her, and I felt horrible for saying it. I realized later in life that my mother was just trying to get me to realize what was best for me because she just wanted the best for me. My perception at the time, however, was something different. I now truly believe she did the best she could with what she knew and how she was brought up. It took becoming a mother myself to understand my mother better. I never met her mother when I was a child because she passed away when I was only seven months old, so I didn't know if she was much like her mother. I just knew I wanted to be a little different from my mother and have my daughter feel she could talk with me about anything and have a hug or kiss any time she needed one.

I think that as most children are turning into adults, they feel they didn't necessarily get all that they wanted from their parents. I believe that's a necessary part of the "cutting the umbilical cord", breaking away from the parents to become their own person. Maybe the parents were too strict and didn't show enough affection, or maybe they didn't say positive things when a child needed to hear them. I think children can easily feel abandonment issues sometimes, if the parents were gone for a short period of time and the child didn't understand why, for example. Little needs can still leave big gaps, even scars, in a person's psyche. And children don't have the vocabulary to state their needs; and most parents aren't taught about abandonment. I know I wasn't.

I recently learned from a relationships class Rand and I attended at our spiritual home, the Center for Spiritual Living, something that I had never heard before. All people need the following five things when they are growing up to have healthy relationships as adults: acceptance, appreciation, affection, allowing and attention. Wow! If they feel they did not receive any or all of these, people will need these very much in their partner relationships. In other words, we all need all these things. If we feel we are lacking in any one of these, we could have issues over this lack – until we find a way to fulfill that need ourselves or can ask a partner for help with that need. Facing that need is a huge step.

WHAT'S THE ANSWER?

I found this information so incredibly simple yet so critical to our psychological well-being. I'm sure Mari would say that she did not have all these needs met. She certainly didn't receive acceptance, affection and attention from her father. She didn't receive acceptance from her friends in high school. She might even feel she didn't get all these things from me.

And then there's guilt. I would say that I have carried guilt over from my childhood into my parenting life, big time. God knows the Catholic church has a market on guilt. I don't regret my Catholic upbringing, not by any means. It gave me a strong moral background. It gave me a foundation of honesty, love, compassion and a true concept of treating everyone as you would want to be treated. I've just moved on, and more openly, to my spirituality which has awakened me to who I am as a loving being. But it's been very hard for me to let go of guilt. And what has that guilt done for me, or for Mari? Did it really accomplish anything? It has never been healthy. It just kept those experiences of our past, packed away – nice and neat – in our baggage! I decided when Mari was living her own life, even before she had her own children, that I could no longer carry that baggage of guilt. It was no longer serving Mari or me.

I recently met a woman with whom I discussed writing this book. I told her what it was about and what my concerns were.

She had similar issues that she had experienced over the years with her now-adult daughter. She was touched by the fact that she had similar fears, guilt and pain and was so grateful that I had given her some ideas and hope. That connection and recognition was integral for me to get to this point. I hope I can do that for others. It's a soul-searching adventure for parents, especially when our children are not who they would like to be and are not happy within. We can only do so much to lead them, guide them, and hope they will take that guidance to heart and learn how to be who they want to be, who they are meant to be – and, be happy with themselves. What have I done? Did I raise her right? What have I learned? I'm still learning. More is always revealed. I tried my best with what I knew at the time. But isn't that a cliché? Is it a cop-out? It could be a cop-out if I'm not totally honest with myself about how much I truly tried to be a good mother.

I loved my daughter, as I do now. I love her heart and soul. She was my whole life for many years. I did not love her any less when I married. Mari is a brilliant, beautiful, honest woman with a loving, loyal and sensitive heart. She has been hurt, many times. She has wanted to die, many times. But she picks herself up and keeps on going, being driven by her love for her children.

WHAT'S THE ANSWER?

When I felt alone and down, even if my downs were not as serious as hers, I kept on going for her.

I recently asked my grandchildren, Mari's beautiful and very mature children, to answer some questions for me about how they felt about themselves and their lives now. They seem very happy with themselves and their lives. They are very smart, honest and honorable young adults. They appreciate what they have and know that they are very lucky to have the lives they are living. They love their parents, even though they've been raised by their parents in separate homes most of their lives. The two oldest are adjusting to becoming adults. And they're doing an incredible job. The youngest child is becoming a fantastic athlete and honor student. They have great memories of their childhoods. They are wonderful children. And they are self-confident.

I've heard that what your children become is a sign of how they were raised. This brings me to the realization that if I raised a child who has always been an honest, loving, caring human being, and her children are just that as well, then maybe I did something right. I believe so.

I asked Mari, as a part of writing about our relationship in this book, how she felt about our relationship now. She feels it's on the mend. She said, "Sometimes it still feels strained, almost strange like." She felt years of distance between us. I can see that. I think if I wasn't always there, physically, when she wanted me to be, she took that as letting her down.

And when I asked her how she felt spiritually, she answered, "lost". I want to help her with that because I believe that could be her answer to happiness – reaching into her soul and knowing how she is loved, as she is. It was what saved me from my pain and difficult times as I was looking for answers in my life, especially when I was raising Mari by myself. The words to a song I heard one Sunday at the Center for Spiritual Living made me cry as I thought of Mari. I want Mari to know who she is as a divine being:

All of me, designed to perfection.

All of me, beautiful and sacred.

All of me, a wonder, expression of the infinite.

All of me, pure light, divine. ~ By Amber Darland

I know she is not happy. I don't think she has ever been happy, or at least like she'd hoped to be. She has been betrayed, abused, and abandoned by people she thought she could trust. She thought they loved her, and then they left her. The first was her father, and that may be the deepest wound of all.

Because she still does not know, deep in her heart, how much she deserves to be happy and have the very best, she is still unhappy. She has carried her pain around with her for forty-seven years. I sob now as I write this. The number one thing a parent will say, when asked by anyone, "What do you want for your child?", will be, "I want my child to be happy."

WHAT'S THE ANSWER?

God intends for us to be happy, just as every parent intends this for his or her child.

I will never give up on her. I can only ask for her forgiveness for not being there for her when she needed me. I can show her how to forgive those who have harmed her. And this forgiveness must go both ways to the ones who harmed you, and yourself. I recently heard someone say that if you're still carrying anger about someone that hurt you in the past, it's like carrying poison in your body and expecting the other person to die. Quite powerful!

I also have talked with her about how I've realized, over the years, that I've deserved to be happy. I've worked hard to bring happiness in my life. I've also learned that I am accountable for everything that occurs in my life, whether things appear to be good or bad. I am not, and will never be, a victim. It's a determination I've always had, all my life. This has given me the power and strength to deal with life's difficulties, allowing me at times to realize that some things may look like the worst experiences of my life – and they actually turn out to be the best things. This is an empowering factor in my life. As I know I have the power to choose how I see a situation in my life – as good or bad, positive or negative – I am creating my life in every moment. We all have choice, in every single moment, to choose to see the positive or negative of that moment. My belief is that I deserve good, positive things in my life; and I trust that I am constantly co-creating these situations, with God, in every moment of my life.

That's incredibly empowering. It's a God-given gift in every single human being. What we believe, we conceive.

I can only hope that Mari can see this, and own it; and that this will, hopefully, allow her to let go of the pain. I believe when she learns to do this, she will have a whole new energy and inner strength she has never felt before. And then she can love herself. If I can finally get Mari to see that, then my work as a parent is done. If I've helped her to see she has the power within her, then I will feel I have raised her right.

Some of the things I've learned in raising my daughter, whether I've raised her right or not, are:

I don't need to fix everything for my child. I cannot do that. Only she can fix her life. I just need to be there for her and listen and, sometimes, advise her.

I did the best I could as a parent, with what I knew at the time.

I had to explain to her that it was never her fault that people hurt her. She should never feel guilt or shame for being assaulted.

Her father has never been there for her, and probably will never be. This is his fault, not hers.

I must be calm, yet firm, in conversations with my child. Again, I must realize I cannot fix her life for her.

If she feels I'm at fault for the things that happened to her, let her vent those feelings. Because she feels that way does not mandate that I must take responsibility for them.

WHAT'S THE ANSWER?

Children, even adult children, need boundaries. If I don't create these boundaries, I enable my child to continue her unhealthy behavior. And sometimes there's not a thing I can say or do to get her to see what I'm saying.

It's important to teach my child that she is accountable for everything in her life, even if it looks incredibly horrific. There is a lesson in it. If she can walk through the pain of it, she will come out stronger, wiser and feeling more empowered.

Ask my child what she wants and expects from me. I may not always be able to give her what she wants at the time; but I can certainly do my best to help her, even if I just listen to her.

Maybe I didn't always give her the love, affection and attention she needed at the time, but I always tried to.

I might not always be popular with my child. She may reject me if she doesn't like what I say to her.

Guilt has never done a thing for me or my child. It has only held us in the past, in negative beliefs.

I can only lead her, guide her and hope she takes that information to heart.

I must reemphasize addiction support groups, such as AA, can help her.

I need to supply her with all the spiritual books I can, so that one day she will have a spiritual epiphany and realize the God light she carries within her.

Sometimes I just couldn't handle her pain. It overwhelmed me to see her like that. It broke my heart and I felt helpless.

I must tell my child how much I love her and always have.

I can love her yet leave her to realize when she is addictive and does not want to help herself.

I can hope and pray that she will love herself and be happy. I cannot make her happy.

She is a beautiful, loving, honest person; and she has raised her three children to be the same. I did raise her right.

ACKNOWLEDGMENTS

Rev. Dr. Andrea Asebedo, Senior Minister,
The Center for Spiritual Living, Bellingham, WA
Amber Darland, Singer and Songwriter,
The Center for Spiritual Living, Bellingham, WA
Candee Blanc and Jes Stone,
The Village Books Publishing Team, Bellingham, WA
Lauren Phillips, Author and Editor, Bellingham, WA
Becky Moore, Healer and Educator, Seattle, WA
Stephanie Morrison, VP-Human Resources, Dallas, TX
Brennon Reed-Henderson, Cover Artist, Seattle, WA
Annabelle Barrett, Book Designer, Bellingham, WA
Richelle Reed, Advisor and Contributor, Seattle, WA
David Richo, Author, How to be an Adult in Relationships
Charlotte Sessoms, Entrepreneur, Bellingham, WA

ABOUT THE AUTHOR

Savannah Moore Stein is a pen name for this first-time author, offering her memoir. Prior to retiring, she had a varied career in telecommunications, interior design and redesign, and caregiving. Following her spiritual path, she has always felt the longing to be a spiritual teacher and public speaker, as a mentor and example to others. Savannah has one adult biological child (about whom this book is written), five adult step-children, one 'other daughter' who is just as much a treasured adult daughter as the others, many grandchildren and step-great-grandchildren. She lives happily in the Pacific Northwest with her loving husband, Rand.

www.ingramcontent.com/pod-product-compliance
Lightning Source LLC
Chambersburg PA
CBHW070302010526
44108CB00039B/1586